Publication Date: January 2004
Info: paula@writers.com

The WORD Book
from Writers.com

A Guide to
Misused,
Misunderstood,
and Confusing
Words
with Bonus Quirky Tangents
& Illuminating Quotations

Paula Guran

writers.com books

The Word Book from Writers.com: A Guide to Misused, Misunderstood, and Confusing Words with Bonus Quirky Tangents & Illuminating Quotations.

Copyright ©2004 by Paula Guran

For more information about Writers On the Net or to subscribe to our monthly newsletter for writers: http://www.writers.com or e-mail writers@writers.com

Manufactured in the United States of America

ISBN 0-9742907-0-X

Published by Writers On the Net/Writers.com
Publishing Office:
87 South Meadowcroft Drive
Akron, Ohio 44313-7266
Educational/Administration Office: Taos, New Mexico

Library of Congress Control Number: 2003110893

Quantity discounts are available on purchases of this book for educational, business, promotional, or special sale purposes.

Contents

To Erik
(autographs supplied free of charge)
and Andrew
(à l'avenir, un immortel de l'Académie française)

ॐ*Preface*ॐ

I'm not an expert on the English language. If they licensed language users, I'd probably have trouble getting a learner's permit. I don't always know what is "right," but I'm pretty good at checking up on myself when I'm unsure of something.

In fact, I may be a little *too* thorough when it comes to checking. I look up an answer and that answer leads to another and those answers lead to interesting information and that information is sometimes contrary to the initial information and some answers contradict other answers and so on and so on and...

This is not entirely due to my autodidactic thirst for knowledge. There is often more than one "right" answer. Sometimes the answer or answers are too convoluted to condense into a single all-encompassing rule. Not that experts do much rule setting of any kind these days. They observe, analyze, and describe. This is a Good Thing. The sources we look to for guidance now explain more and are more accurate with those explanations.

Up until about 100 years ago, though, rule setting and condemnation of rule breaking were important functions of language experts. This was, for the most part, also a Good Thing—established grammar and standardized spelling are needed for a language to fully develop. English would never have become as rich and useful as it is without such measures.

I was taught using this "thou shalt/thou shan't" prescriptive method. I understand why—it is easier to teach and easier to learn a single "correct." For many folks—including non-native-speakers just learning English, those who must learn to clarify their communications, many college-level students who never learned (or were never taught) how to write, and third graders—that's still probably the best approach. Learn the rules, stick to them, and you will be able to communicate effectively. But for those who work or play with words, the simple rules taught in grade school or the style in which they've been drilled as adults may not always the sole universal Truth they need to know.

The more we work and play with words, the more we find that language rules resemble civil laws. Language judges, like public judges with real laws, often have different interpretations of word-laws (but there's no Supreme Court to provide a final ruling in matters of English.) There's also a variance in laws as you move from one jurisdiction to another. The more you travel around in English, the more aware you become of these differences. There are even times when laws conflict. Some of the boundaries of the jurisdictions of language are formed by the situations in which we communicate. These many territories of English— intimate chit-chat, business communication, "institutional" language, fiction, journalism, etc.— all use the English language, but what is appropriate for one may not be for another.

Language is constantly changing, too. Change is much faster than the word-laws can keep up when it comes to vocabulary. We cannot help but be aware of constant additions to our personal lexicons. Less apparent, less frequent, and usually much slower change occurs in usage. Unless you are a linguistic legal eagle you may not even know it has occurred.

And, of course, English-writers are constant creative anarchists anyway. Give us rules and we'll break 'em—and then, often as not, expect to be congratulated for being so imaginative and inventive.

You know all this. Right? You know there may be more than one answer, but have neither the time nor inclination to look for several opinions from many sources. What you need, if possible, is a decent opinion, simple answer, or some concise debate. That is one reason for this little book to exist. It offers some simple answers and informed opinions. Sometimes a little (or more than a little) extra information is offered for your edification. (Trust me. I could have added a great deal more to many of the simple entries. It's a small book. I had to stop somewhere.) There's information for times when dictionaries disagree or don't explain enough for you to make your own call. There's even a consideration or two that the experts may not have caught up with yet.

I've been fortunate in having legitimate (more or less) reasons to spend time exploring quirky language paths. *The Word Book from Writers.com* shares some of these meanderings in both general entries and as *Tangents.* (Some entries are more tangential than the *Tangents.*) Readers are sure to discover all sorts of interesting, or at least odd, minutiae. *The Word Book* aims to be entertaining as well as informative.

If you don't care for digressions and have little use for the rest of the information, you will still find some worthwhile quotations in *The Word Book.* Although I couldn't find a quotation to use as an example for every entry, I supplied them when possible. I enjoy the wisdom, wit, and weirdness and thought readers might, too. If forced to devise my own examples, I occasionally slipped in a small fact. When you come across a statement like this (illustrating the word *gorilla*)—"Fewer than 650 mountain gorillas and 40,000 lowland gorillas are left in the world"—it's a fact I found somewhere.

The Word Book from Writers.com is not a dictionary. There's no attempt to give every definition possible. There are often multiple definitions to help you determine usage, but they are far from complete.

The Word Book is not encyclopedic, either. No effort was made to include every single homophone, all the confusing, misunderstood, or misused words in the English language, or even all the mistakes known to be commonly made. As I mentioned before: it's a small book. It had to end somewhere.

The *Word Book from Writers.com* is not the "final word." It may even begin arguments rather than settle them. With English there may be no ultimate authority, but effort has been made to consult a variety of sources and come up with a practical answer or, at least, enough useful information for you to form your own opinion.

Entries are arranged alphabetically, but there's also an index to help you locate information. The *Contents* page lists the *Tangents*.

—₥—

Some books are stories. Others, like this one, have a story behind them.

The Word Book from Writers.com began as information on usage, lists of troublesome words, and quirky little etymology articles written by an admitted word wonk for *Writers.com*, an electronic newsletter for writers.

Writers.com is produced more or less monthly for Writers On the Net, which is also known as Writers.com. *Writers On the Net* has been helping people achieve their writing goals online since 1995. That may not seem like a long time, but in the world of Web instruction it makes it not only a pioneering venture, but also one of the most experienced entities in the field. [You'll find classes, mentoring, and other services available as well as information on our schedule, fees, and instructors on the Web site (www.writers.com). Subscribe to the newsletter on the site or by e-mailing maillist@writers.com.]

The Word Book's first incarnation was as a free e-book written and published to help writers as a whole and bring specific attention to Writers.com (the services, not the newsletter). While folks were downloading thousands of free copies, we decided we'd try "real" publishing. This improved and expanded version of *The Word Book* is our first publication.

Special thanks to Writers On the Net's Mark Dahlby for giving me the chance to produce *Writers.com*, write this book, and work with Writers On the Net. Additional thanks for years of encouragement and (so far) a few months of publishing.

Paula Guran
September 2003
paula@writers.com

"There is a thousand times more value even in polishing the floor as it should be done than in writing twenty books."—*G.I. Gurdjieff*

❧A❧

a / an

The selection of **a** or **an** does not depend on the first letter of what follows—consonant or vowel—but on the *pronunciation* of what follows. Vowel sounds get *an;* consonant sounds get *a.* Vowels, remember, do not necessarily produce a vowel sound. When *u* makes the same sound as the *y* in *you,* then use *a* (as in *a unicorn*). *An* is used before the unsounded *h,* as in *an honest man.* Do you pronounce *history* with the *h* sound? If so, it takes the *a.*

What about acronyms and initialisms? Usage of *a* or *an* is based on how you would normally pronounce it. The North Atlantic Treaty Organization's acronym is NATO and is pronounced *nato* (rhymes with *ray-toe*), so the appropriate article is *a (a NATO spokesperson).* The intialism for NPR (National Public Radio) is pronounced as individual letters—*en-pee-are*—so *an* would be correct *(an NPR spokesperson).*

With newer inventions, it is sometimes difficult to judge what is commonly accepted pronunciation. Is *FAQ* pronounced *fack* or *eff-ay-kyoo?* Is URL a *yoo-are-el* or an *earl?* Since these are still being "settled," a copyeditor would check with the publisher, other experts, and/or the author to reach a decision. *Wired Style: Principles of English Usage in The Digital Age from the Editors of Wired* states that *FAQ* can be pronounced either way and that it is *yoo-are-el* not *earl.* We think it's *a FAQ* and *an URL.*

❐

a lot / allot / "alot"

The phrase **a lot** is informally used to mean "many."

> ❑ **A lot** of people have asked me how short I am. Since my last divorce, I think I'm about $100,000 short.—Mickey Rooney

It can also mean, informally, "much" or "a large amount.

> ❑ **A lot** of pop music is about stealing pocket money from children. —Ian Anderson

The noun **lot** means a number of things including:

⇨

○ Something, like a slip of paper, used to decide a question. (*We drew **lots** to decide who would pull the trigger.*)

○ The method used to decide. (*The executioner was chosen by **lot**.*)

○ Fate. (*He accepted his **lot** in life without protest.*)

○ A parcel of land. (*The body was found hidden in the underbrush of the vacant **lot**.*)

○ A film studio area. (*We filmed it entirely on the "small town" set on the back lot at Warner.*)

There is no such word as "alot." It should be either two words, as used above, or, if you mean "distribute or give out," it is one word spelled *allot*.

❑ The founders of a new colony... have invariably recognized it among their earliest practical necessities to **allot** a portion of the virgin soil as a cemetery, and another portion as the site of a prison.
—Nathaniel Hawthorne

❐

a while / awhile

The phrase **a while** consists of an article plus a noun. It is usually used after the preposition *for*.

❑ There are cases in which a veil should be drawn **for a while** over liberty.—Montesquieu

Awhile (single word) is an adverb meaning "for a time."

❑ Pause **awhile**,
And let my counsel sway you in this case.—William Shakespeare

❐

aberrant / abhorrent

Aberrant means "different from the typical or acceptable."

❑ What was wrong with communism wasn't **aberrant** leadership, it was communism.—William F. Buckley Jr.

Abhorrent means "extremely offensive."

❑ There is no heresy or no philosophy which is so **abhorrent** to the church as a human being.—James Joyce

❐

abjure / adjure

Abjure means "to solemnly reject or renounce; to avoid."

❑ Graves at my command
Have waked their sleepers, oped, and let 'em forth
By my so potent art.
But this rough magic
I here **abjure**.—William Shakespeare

Adjure means "to ask solemnly or urge earnestly."

❑ I have from an early age **adjured** the use of meat, and the time will
come when men such as I will look upon the murder of animals as they
now look upon the murder of men.—Leonardo da Vinci

❐

adapt / adept

Adapt means "to adjust" or "cause to conform."

❑ Man is an animal who more than any other can **adapt** himself to all
climates and circumstances.—Henry David Thoreau

Adept, when used as an adjective, means "proficient" or "skilled."

❑ I needs must turn
To know what prints I leave, whether of feet,
Or spoor of pads, or a bird's **adept** splay.—Philip Larkin

When **adept** is used as a noun, it refers to "one who is an expert" or "one who
has attained proficiency."

❑ In literature the ambition of the novice is to acquire the literary
language: the struggle of the **adept** is to get rid of it.
—George Bernard Shaw

❐

adverse / averse

Adverse usually refers to things that are contrary or hostile to the subject's interests. *Adverse* normally does not refer to people. *Things* are *adverse*:

- ❑ I didn't like the play, but then I saw it under **adverse** conditions—the curtain was up.—Groucho Marx

- ❑ The spirit of this country is totally **adverse** to a large military force. —Thomas Jefferson

- ❑ One of the duties of the State is that of caring for those of its citizens who find themselves the victims of such **adverse** circumstances as makes them unable to obtain even the necessities for mere existence without the aid of others....—Franklin D. Roosevelt

Averse does refer to *people* (as well as, poetically at least, cats and farmhouses, and philosophically, God). A person who is *averse* to something strongly dislikes it or is opposed to it.

- ❑ God is not **averse** to deceit in a holy cause.—Aeschylus

- ❑ What female heart can gold despise?
  What cat's **averse** to fish?—Thomas Gray

- ❑ The farmhouse lingers, though **averse** to square
  With the new city street it has to wear...—Robert Frost

❐

advice / advise

Advice is the noun.

- ❑ The **advice** of their elders to young men is very apt to be as unreal as a list of the hundred best books.—Oliver Wendell Holmes

Advise is the verb.

- ❑ The physician can bury his mistakes, but the architect can only **advise** his clients to plant vines.—Frank Lloyd Wright

❐

affect / effect

Affect (pronounced *a-FECT*), when used as a verb, means "to influence or make a difference."

❑ Gifts must **affect** the receiver to the point of shock.—Walter Benjamin

Affect (*pronounced AFF-ect*) can be used to mean "emotion," as used by psychiatrists, psychologists, and social scientists. Unless writing in those fields, it is best avoided in everyday usage.

Effect, when used as a verb, means "to cause" or "bring about."

❑ Frankly, I do not know how to **effect** a permanency in American foreign policy.—Franklin D. Roosevelt

When used as a noun, **effect** means "result."

❑ Power is poison. Its **effect** on Presidents had always been tragic. —Henry Brooks Adams

Special effects are used in the movies. Moveable belongings for personal use are **personal effects**.

❒

afflict / inflict

You **afflict** someone *with* punishment or other torments.

❑ The gods being always close to men perceive those who **afflict** others with unjust devices and do not fear the wrath of heaven.—Hesiod

You **inflict** punishment or other torments *on* [*upon*] someone.

❑ There is no kind of harassment that a man may not **inflict** on a woman with impunity in civilized societies.—Denis Diderot

❒

aid / aide

Aid means "help" or "support."

❑ Fortune cannot **aid** those who do nothing.—Sophocles

Aide means an "assistant" or a "helper."

❑ Divine right went out with the American Revolution and doesn't belong to the White House **aides**. What meat do they eat that makes them grow so great?—Sam Ervin

Neither **aid** nor **aide** are used as a suffix when referring to a sweet drink like lemonade or limeade. *Kool-Aid* is a registered trademark for the instant fruit-flavored beverage product.

❐

aisle / isle

An **aisle** is a passageway.

❑ Where through the long-drawn **aisle** and fretted vault,
The pealing anthem swells the note of praise.—Thomas Gray

An **isle** is a poetic reference to island or a small island.

❑ This royal throne of kings, this sceptred **isle**,
This earth of majesty, this seat of Mars...
This blessèd plot, this earth, this realm, this England.
—William Shakespeare

❐

all ready / already

To be **all ready** (two words) is to be prepared.

❑ We are **all ready** to be savage in some cause. The difference between a good man and a bad one is the choice of the cause.—William James

Already can mean "previously."

❑ All the good music has **already** been written by people with wigs and stuff.—Frank Zappa

Already can also informally mean "so soon"; as in *Is it time to go already?*

No, there is no word spelled "*allready*."

❐

all right / "alright"

With "**alright**" and **all right** you are knee-deep in the evolutionary stream of English. Yes, that's the current of change frothing around you. Exciting isn't it? Climb out of the creek and we'll explain.

H.W. Fowler (see *Tangent* below) in his 1926 *Dictionary of Modern English Usage* made no bones about it: "The words should always be written separate; there are no such forms as 'all-right,' 'allright,' or 'alright'...." But haven't we embraced *almighty*, *already*, and *altogether*? What is the objection to *alright?* Those accepted word fusions occurred back in the 13th and 14th centuries when English wasn't even English yet. Folks didn't start trying to fuse *all right* into *alright* until the late 19th century. By then, of course, we had experts and dictionarists and such things could be dealt with before they went too far. (What next? *Alwrong?*)

Let us stress—as far as formal or standard usage goes, *alright* is still not a word. It is beginning to creep into dictionaries under the guise of "acceptable variant," "in reputable use," and "commonly used." Some feel there's an argument to be made for using *alright* to mean "okay"" or "acceptable." This would be in keeping with the distinctions made with all *ready/already* (see above) and *all together/altogether* (see below). Thus, if we wrote *The kids are alright* it would mean they are satisfactory. If we wrote *The kids are all right* it would mean they are—each and every one of them—correct.

But the argument has yet to be won. If you decide to be a word pioneer and use *alright* in your writing many (including us) will consider it an error. Others may see you as a dangerous radical who spits in the eye of established order. Either alternative should probably to be avoided in the world of writing.

❏ I don't have any bad habits. They might be bad for other people, but they're **all right** for me.—Eubie Blake

---

TANGENT: Prescriptive Pretension-Picking Pundit

This is our first reference to Henry Watson Fowler (1858–1933), but not our last.

After 17 years teaching the classics to schoolboys, Fowler joined with his brother, Francis George Fowler, to write what they referred to as "a sort of English composition manual, from the negative point of view, for journalists & amateur writers." The "composition manual" became *The King's English* and, after publication by Oxford University Press, it almost immediately became a standard. *The Concise Oxford Dictionary of Current English* followed in 1911. Military service in World War I and the death of Francis George in 1918 delayed, but did not defeat, Fowler's completion of his major work. *A Dictionary of Modern English Usage* was published in 1926. Fowler's wit, style,

⇨

Tangent (continued)

and capricious idiosyncrasies made the *MEU* delightfully readable for its own sake; his common sense, prescriptive (but invariably pretension-pricking), and conservative advice made it the Bible of English usage. Of course, as William Safire has written, "Fowler wrote the Bible on usage, but *Modern English Usage* needs revision every generation to stay modern." Such is the nature of language. Further, Fowler may have had genius as a lexicographer, but he was not trained as one, nor was he an academic grammarian. (Perhaps this was a great strength rather than a weakness.) We do not always depend on or defend *Fowler* or Fowler (like Webster and Roget, his name has become synonymous with his work), but we appreciate both the books and their writer.

We also try to follow (we do not say we "succeed in following") his advice concerning what it takes to be a "good writer": "Any one who wishes to become a good writer should endeavour, before he allows himself to be tempted by the more showy qualities, to be direct, simple, brief, vigorous, and lucid." Moreover, we realize Mr. Fowler would disapprove of many of our practices—especially our tendency toward quotation—although he may have appreciated our attitude as we quote him anyway:

> A writer expresses himself in words that have been used before because they give his meaning better than he can give it himself, or because they are beautiful or witty, or because he expects them to touch a cord of association in his reader, or because he wishes to show that he is learned and well read. Quotations due to the last motive are invariably ill-advised; the discerning reader detects it and is contemptuous; the undiscerning is perhaps impressed, but even then is at the same time repelled, pretentious quotations being the surest road to tedium.

❒

all together / altogether

Altogether is an adverb meaning "completely, entirely, on the whole."

❑   Hunger is an **altogether** fit companion for the idle man.—Hesiod

All together is a phrase meaning "in a group."

❑   When the day of Pentecost came they were **all together** in one place. —Acts 2:1

❒

all ways / always

The phrase **all ways** (two words) means "by every measure."

❑ To give and then not feel that one has given is the very best of **all ways** of giving.—Max Beerbohm

The adverb **always** means "at all times, continuously."

❑ There is **always** some madness in love. But there is also **always** some reason in madness.—Friedrich Nietzsche

❒

allude / elude

When you **allude** to something you are referring to it indirectly.

❑ He **alludes** to the appearance of a face in the orb of the moon. —Diogenes Laërtius

If you **elude** something you are trying to escape or avoid it.

❑ The want of knowledge annoys. Too much logic bores. Life **eludes** logic, and everything that logic alone constructs remains artificial and forced.—André Gide

❒

allusion / illusion

An **allusion** is an indirect reference.

❑ I think we must quote whenever we feel that the **allusion** is interesting or helpful or amusing.—Cliff Fadiman

An **illusion** is an erroneous belief or perception.

❑ Reality is merely an **illusion**, albeit a very persistent one. —Albert Einstein

❒

altar / alter

An **altar** is a raised place or structure that serves as the central point of worship.

❑ Wherever an **altar** is found, there civilization exists. —Joseph De Maistr

Alter is a verb that means *to change* or *to modify*.

❑ Typography tended to **alter** language from a means of perception and exploration to a portable commodity. —Marshall McLuhan

❒

amok / amuck

Either version is considered acceptable, but the Associated Press prefers **amok**. That's the spelling you'll find most often, usually in the idiom "to run amok," meaning "in a murderously violent frenzy" or, figuratively, "to behave wildly and uncontrollably."

> ❏ Genius as an explosive power beats gunpowder hollow; and if knowledge, which should give that power guidance, is wanting, the chances are not small that the rocket will simply run **amuck** among friends and foes.—Thomas Henry Huxley

---

Tangent: Amok, Hamas & History

Amok came into English from Malay. You may read that *amok* is the "only" word or "one of the few" to be acquired from Malay, but the former is untrue and the veracity of the latter depends on your definition of "few." English words of Malaysian origin include *orangutan, gingham, sarong, bamboo, rattan, kapok, paddy, compound, mango, sago, cassowary, cockatoo, gecko, gutta-percha, rattan,* and *ketchup.* There's also evidence that several words considered to be Chinese in origin—*junk* (the boat), *mandarin, gong, caddy* (a container for tea), and even the word *tea* itself— came from Malay. (We think that's more than "a few.")

Malay may actually have acquired *amok* from an Arabic word, *hamoq,* meaning "uncontrolled, violent, stupid anger." Digressing from our digression for the moment we insert some timely etymology: According to some, there are two opposing words for anger in Arabic, *hamoq* and *hamas,* with the latter meaning "disciplined, controlled, thoughtful anger." *Hamas* is usually defined, however, as "zeal." It derives from the verb *hamisa* and it conveys the idea of throwing one's self wholeheartedly into a cause. In 1987, as an outgrowth of the Palestinian branch of the Muslim Brotherhood, an Islamic political organization was formed that chose *Hamas* as its name. Not only does it mean "zeal" (and, perhaps, "purposeful anger"), it is an acronym for *Harakat al-muqawama al-islamiyya* (Islamic Resistance Movement). (We wonder: as an acronym shouldn't we render it as HAMAS in English?) Hamas, of course, is now known primarily for its adherents who blow themselves up and take as many Israelis as they can with them.

Malaysia acquired more than just a word or two from Arabic-speakers. During the 13th and 14th centuries, Indian and Arab traders brought Islam to the Malay Peninsula. The area had, since around the first century B.C., been heavily influenced by the Chinese and Indian cultures and the Indian Hindu and Buddhist religions. When Parameswara, the Malay-Hindu ruler of the port city of Malacca (now Melaka), was converted to Islam around 1400, Islam became a major influence on the peninsula and

⇨

Tangent (continued)

Arabic-speaking Muslims dominated the lucrative spice trade. (Islam remains today as the state religion of Malaysia.)

The Arabs retained control of the lucrative spice trade for about a century, channeling commodities through Venetian merchants to the rest of Europe. After Vasco de Gama proved there was a viable sea route to India via the Cape of Good Hope (1498), the Portuguese decided to obtain the spices themselves. To gain the upper hand, they captured the important trading port of Malacca, in 1511. The port remained under Portuguese control for 130 years until the Dutch captured it.

Amok entered Portuguese as *amuco* some time before 1516. Its first documented English use (as *amouco*) was 1663. In 1772 Captain James Cook, nicely embodying the Western imperialist tendency to denigrate any culture other than its own, wrote: "To run amock is to get drunk with opium, to sally forth from the house, kill the person or persons supposed to have injured the Amock, and any other person that attempts to impede his passage."

European interpretation of just what *amok* meant varied. William Marsden, an English orientalist, published a definition (in 1812 in his *Grammar and Dictionary of the Malay Language*) defining *amok* as "engaging furiously in battle, attacking with desperate resolution, rushing in a state of frenzy to the commission of indiscriminate murder." (The *Oxford English Dictionary* still cites Marsden's definition.)

Sir Frank Swettenham (1850–1946), who became the first British Resident-General of the Federated Malay State in 1882, saw *amok* as a mental disorder. He wrote (in 1885): "Amok is an exclusively male disorder and occurs more often in rural communities. There is sometimes a prodromal period of brooding before the homicidal outburst but there is usually no previous feeling of hostility towards the victims. The attack endangers the life of the *peng-amok* who is often killed by the villagers or police." Swettenham distinguished between two types of *amok*; one applied to "the onslaught of a body of men in war time, or where plunder is the object and murder the means to arrive at it"; and the other "more commonly used to describe the action of an individual who suddenly and without apparent cause, seizes a weapon and strikes out blindly, killing and wounding all who come in his way, regardless of age or sex, whether they are friends, strangers, or his own nearest relatives."

Swettenham believed "that about sixty per cent of the Malays who *meng-amok* are mentally diseased, usually from inherited causes. Of the rest, what happens is this: some serious trouble overtakes a man (serious to him, that is). He is insulted by a man, jealous of, scorned or rejected by a woman—and the times are out of joint. He broods over his trouble

⇨

Tangent (continued)

and says, 'I shan't be able to put up with this, I must *meng-amok*'. He thinks this is the only dignified way of getting out of his trouble, the only course sanctioned by ancient custom."

Walter W. Skeat (1835–1912), a great English philologist (who wrote the standards *The Principles of English Etymology* and *Etymological English Dictionary* as well as *Malay Magic*), saw *amok* as "the Malay national method of committing suicide, especially as one never hears of Malays committing suicide in any other way. This form of suicide may arise from a wish to die fighting and thus avoid a 'straw death, a cow's death'..."

One way or another, the English meaning involves being crazed, frenzied, or out of control, but the Malaysian meaning, at least originally, is quite different. Studying the meaning of *amok* using classical Malay sources, linguist Hazidi Abdul Hamid of the Universiti Kebangsaan Malaysia, found that *amok* may include violence, but there's nothing uncontrolled or crazy about it.

In an article written in 2001, Hamid explains that in classical Malay, *amok* is an emotional state in which a person causes hurt to others, but that person is not wildly out of control. The person in *amok* is in control of mental faculties and one can even be invited to join in *amok* or be commanded, in the military sense, to prepare for and go into an *amok*.

❐

amoral / immoral / nonmoral / unmoral

Amoral refers to being neither moral nor *immoral;* without or not caring about standards of behavior.

❑ I am fond of music I think because it is so **amoral**. Everything else is moral and I am after something that isn't. I have always found moralizing intolerable.—Hermann Hesse

Immoral refers to the violation of established moral principles.

❑ It is **immoral** to get drunk because the headache comes after the drinking, but if the headache came first and the drunkenness afterwards, it would be moral to get drunk.—Samuel Butler

Nonmoral and **unmoral** are also words. **Unmoral** is usually defined as or closely synonymous with *amoral* (and sometimes *nonmoral*). **Nonmoral** commonly means "not falling into or existing in the sphere of morals or ethics," but may have other meanings in the context of ethical morality and philosophical discourse. We caution the use of either *nonmoral* or *unmoral* by most writers as they may be construed as mistakes or nonstandard.

❐

among / amongst

There is no real difference of sense or function between the two. **Amongst** seems to be somewhat less common in American English than in British English.

- ❑ If a politician found he had cannibals **among** his constituents, he would promise them missionaries for dinner.—H. L. Mencken

- ❑ The greatest vicissitude of things **amongst** men is the vicissitude of sects and religions.—Francis Bacon

❒

among / between

We're sure your English teacher taught you that **among** is used for three or more and **between** is used when the choice involves exactly two. We advise you to stick with the rule in formal writing, but we also note it's not quite that cut and dried. **Between** is used when the units involved define the borders of an area, its limits, or the endpoints of a range:

- ❑ Alexander the Great conquered all the land **between** Greece, India, and Egypt.

- ❑ She had not exactly remained chaste **between** any of her marriages.

Between is also used when the units involved are regarded as individual entities

- ❑ Diplomatic relations **between** Great Britain, France, and Germany [or **between** some members of the EEC] were strained by the final vote.

❒

annual / annul

Annual means "yearly."

- ❑ **Annual** income twenty pounds, **annual** expenditure nineteen nineteen six, result happiness. **Annual** income twenty pounds, **annual** expenditure twenty pounds ought and six, result misery.
  —Charles Dickens

To **annul** means "to void."

- ❑ In order not to **annul** our free will, I judge it true that Fortune may be mistress of one half our actions but then even she leaves the other half, or almost, under our control.— Niccolo Machiavelli

❒

any one / anyone

The phrase **any one** means "any single person or thing." It is usually followed by "of." (Although it isn't in our example.)

❑ Twelve significant photographs in **any one** year is a good crop. —Ansel Adams

The pronoun **anyone** means "any person at all; anybody."

❑ **Anyone** who considers protocol unimportant has never dealt with a cat.—Robert A. Heinlein

❐

any way / anyway / "anyways"

The words **any way** mean "any method."

❑ Increase of material comforts, it may be generally laid down, does not in **any way** whatsoever conduce to moral growth.—Mohandas Gandhi

Anyway is an adverb meaning "anyhow, nevertheless, in any case."

❑ You're dead if you aim only for kids. Adults are only kids grown up **anyway**.—Walt Disney

Anyways is grammatically incorrect, although often used in colloquial speech.

❐

appraise / apprise

The verb **appraise** means "to ascertain value."

❑ When one cannot **appraise** out of one's own experience, the temptation to blunder is minimized, but even when one can, appraisal seems chiefly useful as appraisal of the appraiser.—Marianne Moore

The verb **apprise** means "to inform or notify."

❑ It affords me sincere pleasure to be able to **apprise** you of the entire removal of the Cherokee Nation of Indians to their new homes west of the Mississippi.—Martin van Buren

❐

ascent / assent

Ascent is the act of going upward (ascending).

❑ The delights of this life are not its own, but our fear of the **ascent** into a higher life; the torments of this life are not its own, but our self-torment because of that fear.—Franz Kafka

Ascent can also mean "an upward slope."

❑ And full against the steep **ascent** I set
My face, where highest to Heaven its top o'erflows.—Dante Alighieri

Assent means "to agree."

❑ You can get **assent** to almost any proposition so long as you are not going to do anything about it.—John Jay Chapman

assistance / assistants

Assistance is the aid offered.

❑ If men had to do their vile work without the **assistance** of woman and the stimulant of strong drink they would be obliged to be more divine and less brutal.—Caroline Nichols Churchill

Assistants are helpers.

❑ I don't like to work with **assistants**. I'm already one too many; the camera alone would be enough.—Alfred Eisenstaedt

assure / ensure / insure

Assure means "to guarantee."

❑ We are persons of quality, I **assure** you, and women of fashion, and come to see and to be seen.—Ben Jonson

Ensure means "to make sure."

❑ Health, learning and virtue will **ensure** your happiness; they will give you a quiet conscience, private esteem and public honour.
—Thomas Jefferson

Insure means "to protect against loss."

❑ To **insure** good health: eat lightly, breathe deeply, live moderately, cultivate cheerfulness, and maintain an interest in life.
—William Londen

aural / oral

Aural means "relating to hearing or the ear."

❑ [M]ost of those who buy my records are listening in on others' conversation. They are the **aural** equivalent of voyeurs, thrilled at this crazy world that has nothing to do with their experience.
—Ice-T [Tracy Marrow]

Oral refers to spoken words. (Also see entry for *oral/verbal*.)

❑ My opposition [to interviews] lies in the fact that offhand answers have little value or grace of expression, and that such **oral** give and take helps to perpetuate the decline of the English language.—James Thurber

❏

awake/ awaken / wake / waken

All four words mean about the same thing—"to emerge from sleep; to be alert." Some suggest that **waken** be used only transitively (as in *The morning light wakened her*) and **awaken** only intransitively (as in *She awakened at the sound of the alarm*), but transitive *(She woke up the entire household)* and intransitive *(They are waking up)* senses are well established for both.

Awake and **awaken** are often considered "old-fashioned" or "more formal," although they are still commonly used in written English—especially in a figurative *(Crimes awake the town's fears)* or poetic *(His touch awakened her soul)* sense.

Wake or **wake up** are used much more often in daily speech than *awake* and *awaken*. When asking or commanding, *wake up* is the norm. *To wake* is almost always a phrasal verb, accompanied by *up*. (The exception being when *wake* is used in the context of keeping watch before a burial.)

❑ Each morning when I **awake**, I experience again a supreme pleasure— that of being Salvador Dali.—Salvador Dali

❑ That one individual should **awaken** in another memories that belong to still a third is an obvious paradox.—Jorge Luis Borges

❑ One short sleep past, we **wake** eternally,
And Death shall be no more; Death, thou shalt die!—John Donne

❑ I like to **wake up** each morning feeling a new man.—Jean Harlow

❑ The law is not thrust upon man; it rests deep within him, to **waken** when the call comes.—Martin Buber

❏

❧ B ❧

bail / bale

Bail is the security given for release from jail. (There are many other definitions connected with this meaning.)

❑ Get jailed, jump **bail**
Join the army if you fail—Bob Dylan

Bail also means "to scoop water out of something."

❑ The boat was taking on water, so we had to **bail**.

The phrase **bail out**, as in making a parachute jump, and the colloquial expression **bail out**, as in rescue from a situation, both come from this meaning.

A **bale** is a large, closely bound bundle.

❑ The hay was collected together and compressed into a **bale**.

TANGENT: Hail Bail!

As noted above, *bail* has many meanings associated with posting something of value in order to get out of jail. We discovered it had many other meanings *not* associated with going to the hoosegow. Here are some of them:

❍ A semicircular support as on a covered wagon.

❍ A handle for a pail.

❍ The bar with rollers that holds paper in place on a typewriter

❍ In Australia and New Zealand, a bail is a framework that holds the head of a cow during milking.

❍ In the game of cricket: either of two crosspieces bridging the stumps (the three upright pieces) of a wicket.

Feel free to drop any of these into your next conversation or crossword puzzle. No need to credit us.

❏

baited / bated

Baited means enticed lured or tormented

- ❑ Keep thy hook always **baited**, for a fish lurks ever in the most unlikely swim.—Ovid

Bated is the past tense of the verb *bate*, but you may never have heard *bate* used except as *bated* and in the idiom "with bated breath." You are more likely to be familiar with the verb *abate* and know it means "to lessen, subside, diminish" or (in law) "to nullify or void." *Abate* became *bate* through a phonetic process called "aphesis"—the loss of a short, usually unstressed, vowel or syllable at the beginning of a word. (Other aphetic examples include *lone* from *alone, squire* from *esquire,* and *cute* from *acute.*) Although *bate* lost the *a* of *abate,* it retained the same basic meaning. When you wait with bated breath you are in a state of such suspenseful anticipation that you almost stop breathing—as in our example from *Tom Sawyer:*

- ❑ Every eye fixed itself upon him; with parted lips and **bated** breath the audience hung upon his words, taking no note of time, rapt in the ghastly fascinations of the tale—Mark Twain

bare / bear

Bare means "exposed to view."

- ❑ **Bare** woods, whose branches strain,
  Deep caves and dreary main,—
  Wail, for the world's wrong.—Percy Bysshe Shelley

Bear can mean:

○ Carry or transport.

- ❑ ...**bear** my greeting to the senators
  And tell them that I will not come today.—William Shakespeare

○ Tolerate, stand or endure.

- ❑ I could never **bear** to be buried with people to whom I had not been introduced.—Norman Parkinson

○ A large mammal.

- ❑ The grizzly **bear** whose potent hug
  Was feared by all, is now a rug.—Arthur Guiterman

base / bass / bass

Base (pronounced to rhyme with *face*) has several meanings. Among the most common:

○ Bottom part which supports that above it.

❏ All love that has not friendship for its **base**,
Is like a mansion built upon the sand.—Ella Wheeler Wilcox

○ Worthless, inferior, morally low.

❏ I have always heard, Sancho, that doing good to **base** fellows is like throwing water into the sea.—Miguel de Cervantes

○ A main place.

❏ Houston, Tranquillity **Base** here. The Eagle has landed.
—Neil A. Armstrong

○ In baseball, any one of four corners of the infield.

❏ Lou Brock was a great **base** stealer but today I am the greatest.
—Rickey Henderson

Bass (pronounced like *base*) means "deep or low in sound."

❏ Under the man-of-war scourge, curses mix with tears; and the sigh and the sob furnish the **bass** to the shrill octave of those who laugh to drown buried griefs of their own—Herman Melville

A **bass** can also be an instrument.

❏ Dragonetti was a 19th century double **bass** virtuoso.

Bass (when pronounced to rhyme with *mass*) is a type of fish.

❏ She had rouged her cheeks to a color otherwise seen only on specially ordered Pontiac Firebirds, and in her ears she wore two feathered appliances resembling surfcasting jigs especially appetizing to striped **bass**.—George V. Higgins

❐

bazaar / bizarre

A **bazaar** is a marketplace.

❑ The traditional Persian **bazaar** was the commercial and financial center of a city.

If something is **bizarre** it is very odd.

❑ Old women snore violently. They are like bodies into which **bizarre** animals have crept at night; the animals are vicious, bawdy, noisy. —Joyce Carol Oates

berth / birth

A **berth** can be enough room for a ship to maneuver, a place to sleep, a position, or a place to dock a ship or park a vehicle. (The colloquial phrase, *a wide berth*, means "a safe distance.")

❑ When, within a fortnight of my brother's sailing, I heard that MacCoy had taken a **berth** in the Etruria, I was as certain as if he had told me that he was going over to England for the purpose of coaxing Edward back again into the ways that he had left.—Arthur Conan Doyle

Birth has to do with the act or event of being born. It can also mean "the time when something begins."

❑ You must have chaos within you to give **birth** to a dancing star. —Friedrich Nietzsche

bimonthly / biweekly / semimonthly / semiweekly

❑ A **bimonthly** event takes place once every two months.

❑ A **biweekly** event takes place once every two weeks.

❑ A **semimonthly** event is held twice a month.

❑ A **semiweekly** event occurs twice a week.

❑ In publishing, a **bimonthly** comes out every two months and a **biweekly** every two weeks.

Tip: So many people are confused by these words, the best way to be absolutely clear might be to substitute expressions such as "every two months" or "twice a month."

bloc / block

A **bloc** is a group with a shared purpose.

❑ Are we all clear that we want to build something that can aspire to be a world power—not just a trading **bloc**, but a political entity? —Romano Prodi

Block, with a *k,* means:

○ A chunk, a portion.

❑ What sculpture is to a **block** of marble, education is to an human soul.—Joseph Addison

❑ The skyscraper establishes the **block**, the **block** creates the street, the street offers itself to man.—Roland Barthes

○ Hinder.

❑ A good dog does not **block** the road.—Chinese proverb

❏

blond / blonde (see also *brunet / brunette*)

The Associated Press Stylebook settles the question with: "Use *blond* as a noun for males and an adjective for all applications: She has *blond* hair. Use *blonde* as a noun for females." But, really, it is not quite that cut and blow-dried.

Blond and *blonde* came into English from French. This once meant that, in the French manner, the adjective or noun *blonde* was used when referring to a female; *blond* used when referring to a male. But there's considerable history of the non-gendered noun *blond* being used for women as well as men. Further complicating an easy answer: whether we write *A blond walked by* or *A blonde walked by*, most people will assume a female walked by. (Tsk. We live in a sexist society.) Avoid sexism by using *blond* only as an adjective that modifies hair (or an equivalent) rather than a person. All that being said, we feel there are times when calling a woman with *blonde* or *blond* hair *a blonde* intentionally conveys a great deal in a very clear manner:

❑ **Blondes** make the best victims. They're like virgin snow that shows up the bloody footprints.—Alfred Hitchcock

❑ It was a **blonde**. A **blonde** to make a bishop kick a hole in a stained glass window.—Raymond Chandler

❑ The hippies wanted peace and love. We wanted Ferraris, **blondes** and switchblades.—Alice Cooper

❑ I'm not offended by dumb **blonde** jokes because I know that I'm not dumb. I also know I'm not **blonde**.—Dolly Parton

❏

boarder / border

A **boarder** is a lodger who receives regular meals.

- ❑ The widow took in a **boarder** to help make ends meet.

A **border** is a boundary.

- ❑ Good evening Mr. and Mrs. America, from **border** to **border** and coast to coast and all the ships at sea. Let's go to press.—Walter Winchell

❐

bolder / boulder

To be **bolder** is to be more daring.

- ❑ If I could dwell
  Where Israfel
      Hath dwelt, and he were I,
  He might not sing so wildly well
      A mortal melody,
  While a **bolder** note than this might swell
      From my lyre within the sky.—Edgar Allan Poe

A **boulder** a large rock.

- ❑ Let the gentle bush dig its root deep and spread upward to split the **boulder**.— Carl Sandburg

Tip: The name of the city in Colorado is **Boulder**.

❐

born / borne

Born means "to be brought into existence."

- ❑ A man may be **born**, but in order to be **born** he must first die, and in order to die he must first awake.—G.I. Gurdjieff

Borne, with an *e,* means:

○ Carried.

- ❑ The burden which is well **borne** becomes light.—Ovid

○ Tolerated.

- ❑ All sorrows can be **borne** if you put them into a story or tell a story about them.—Isak Dinesen

❐

brake / break

A **brake** is a device that helps you stop.

❑ The wheel and the **brake** have different duties, but also one in common: to hurt one another.—Friedrich Nietzsche

A **break** is a rupture, fracture, or crack.

❑ You will soon **break** the bow if you keep it always stretched.—Phaedrus

breach / breech

A **breach** is a gap or the act of breaking a promise, agreement, law, relationship

❑ Once more into the **breach**, dear friends, once more; Or close the wall up with our English dead!—William Shakespeare

Breech means "hind end" (thus a **breech birth** or the **breech of a gun**).

❑ [Sir Michael Tippett's large-scale choral work *The Mask of Time*] resembles a **breech** delivery—one which is expressed in rhythmic lurches, stabs of phrase and vocal ornamentation designed to express agitation rather than decorative grace.—Bernard Holland

breath / breathe

Breath is respiration.

❑ A human being is only **breath** and shadow.—Sophocles

Breathe is when you inhale and exhale.

❑ Argument is to me the air I **breathe**. Given any proposition, I cannot help believing the other side and defending it.—Gertrude Stein

Tip: If you are referring to width or broadness, the word you want is **breadth**.

❑ Lepidus: What manner o' thing is your crocodile?
Antony: It is shaped, sir, like itself, and it is as broad as it hath **breadth**.—William Shakespeare

bridal / bridle

Bridal has to do with a bride or wedding.

❑ Quarrels often arise in marriages when the **bridal** gifts are excessive. —Decimus Magnus Ausonius

Bridle means:

○ The headgear used to control a horse.

❑ Reason lies between the **bridle** and the spur.—Italian proverb

○ To restrain or control.

❑ You can no more **bridle** passions with logic than you can justify them in the law courts. Passions are facts and not dogmas.—Alexander Herzen

---

Tangent: Brides & Grooms

This set of homonyms made us wonder about the word **bridegroom**. A **groom** takes care of a horse. *Bridles* are used to control horses. Why would a *bride* have a *groom?*

The word *bridegroom* proved to be a good example of *folk* (or *popular*) *etymology*. The term refers to a process that occurs when a word is "lost" or acquired from a foreign language and is then modified into something more familiar. In the 17th century, for instance, the Spanish word *cucaracha* was altered by English-speakers to become *cockroach*. *Woodchuck* was an adaptation from the Cree word *wuchak* (or something close to it, English speakers spelled—and probably pronounced—it several ways). *Cellar* in the phrase *salt cellar* was originally *saler* and came from the French *salière*, "a salter."

This is the way folk etymology worked with *bridegroom* according to John Ayto and others: Before 1066 (the Old English era) the word was **bryd-guma**: *bryd=bride, guma=man*. (*Guma* descended from the Latin for "man," *homo*.) By the 1200s, *guma* had disappeared as a stand-alone word and *bryd-guma* had survived as *bride-gome*.

The word *groom*, meaning "boy, lad, male servant" appeared, rather mysteriously, at about the same time. There are words with a superficial similarity in Old French and Old Norse, but they cannot be proven to be related. Whatever its source, *groom* became a common word, *gome* was not much used, and *bridegome* became *bridegroom*. (*Groom* did not become associated with taking care of horses until the 17th century.)

❐

broach /brooch

To **broach** is to introduce.

❑ The Prime Minister planned to **broach** the subject with the Queen.

A **brooch** is an ornamental pin.

❑ Queen Victoria had the 106 carat Koh-i-noor diamond set in a **brooch**.

❑

bouillon / bullion

Bouillon is a clear seasoned soup

❑ Having your book turned into a movie is like seeing your oxen turned into **bouillon** cubes.—John Le Carré

Bullion is (usually) precious metals formed into bars or ingots.

❑ The gold vault at Fort Knox has held as much as $56 billion worth of gold **bullion**.

❑

brunet / brunette (also see entry for *blond / blonde*)

As we learned with the entry for *blond/blonde,* things would be simplest if we just blindly followed one rule. Of course, that means deciding which rule to follow. The AP's rule for this French duo is the same as for its lighter-hued equivalent: "Use *brunet* as a noun for males, and as the adjective for both sexes. Use *brunette* as the noun for females." But the dark duo is plagued with the same usage problems as the paler pair: females can be *brunet* or *brunette,* but men can never be *brunettes.* Worse, the specter of sexism hangs over the adumbral dyad with even more weight than over the stramineous mates. Think about it: How often do you hear a male referred to as *brunet* at all? Dark-haired, yes; *brunet,* no. In the real world, either spelling almost always refers to females and *brunette* is far more common. Not that popularity alone makes anything right.

Considering popularity, we note (for what it is worth), that the Google search engine lists only 286,000 results for *brunet,* over 3 million for *brunette,* close to 4 million for *blond,* and a staggering 14 million-plus for *blonde.* We caution you not to try this experiment at home as many of the results might cause you to blush to your very roots no matter what color your roots are.

All of this discussion of French hair colors has left us wondering: Why did English pick up *blond, blonde, brunet,* and *brunette* yet not take *roux* and *rousse* or the less proper, *rouquin,* and *rouquine?*

❑

buy / by / bye

Buy means "purchase."

❑ **Buy** good books, and read them; the best books are the commonest, and the last editions are always the best, if the editors are not blockheads.—Philip Dormer Stanhope, 4th Earl Chesterfield

By means "through the action of."

❑ All modern American literature comes from one book by Mark Twain called *Huckleberry Finn.*—Ernest Hemingway

Bye is a short, colloquial form of goodbye.

❑ **Bye**, Toots, you're a swell gal.

Bye can also mean (primarily in sports or games) "advancement to the next round in a tournament without facing an opponent."

❑ Bowlers who draw a **bye** must bowl 190 to earn victory

Idioms using *by*:

❑ **by and by** means "*sooner or later.*"
❑ **by the by** and **by the way** mean "incidentally" or "please note."
❑ **by and large** means "taking everything into consideration."

A Note on *goodbye*: The Associated Press and most editors prefer **goodbye** rather than **good-bye** (with a hyphen), although you will find both hyphenated and unhyphenated versions in the dictionary; **goodby** with no *e* is not considered acceptable.

❐

❧C❧

cache / cash

A **cache** is hidden storage or, in computer terminology, temporary storage.

❑ People allowed maybe old Captain Obed traded for [the queer foreign kind of jewelry] in some heathen port... Others thought and still think he'd found an old pirate **cache** out on Devil Reef.—H.P. Lovecraft

Cash is money in coins or notes.

❑ Better eight hundred in **cash** than a thousand on credit.
—Chinese proverb

callous / callus

Callous means "unfeeling."

❑ It is human to err, and at least no one can accuse you of being a **callous** criminal.—Arthur Conan Doyle

A **callus** is hard, thickened skin.

❑ Most things break, including hearts. The lessons of life amount not to wisdom, but to scar tissue and **callus**.—Wallace Stegner

cannon / canon

Although cannon has other meanings beyond "a big gun," that is the most common.

❑ If they want peace, nations should avoid the pin-pricks that precede **cannon** shots.—Napoleon Bonaparte

Among several meanings for **canon** are "law, criterion, or principle"; "religious dogma"; "a type of priest"; "accepted group of standard creative works."

❑ Art is not the application of a **canon** of beauty but what the instinct and the brain can conceive beyond any **canon**. When we love a woman we don't start measuring her limbs.—Pablo Picasso

canvas / canvass

Canvas is a durable cloth used in tents and sails and upon which an artist paints.

❑ A painter paints pictures on **canvas**. But musicians paint their pictures on silence.—Leopold Stokowski

To **canvass** means:

○ To examine or discuss.

❑ An opinion that we are likely soon to **canvass**.—Sir W. Hamilton

○ To go and solicit orders or political support or to determine opinions.

❑ We were to **canvass** the voters in the ward and report to the mayor.

❐

capital / capitol

Capital can mean:

○ A city where the seat of government of a state or country is located.

❑ All is politics in this **capital**.—Thomas Jefferson

○ An upper case letter.

❑ She lived in **capital** letters.—Al Carmine (eulogy for Marion Tanner, model for Auntie Mame)

○ Money or wealth.

❑ **Capital** is dead labor, which, vampire-like, lives only by sucking living labor, and lives the more, the more labor it sucks.—Karl Marx

○ First-rate, chief; excellent.

❑ Boys are **capital** fellows in their own way, among their mates; but they are unwholesome companions for grown people.—Charles Lamb

A **capitol** is the building or group of buildings where a legislative body meets. When capitalized, **Capitol** means the building in which the U.S. Congress meets in Washington, D.C. or the temple of Jupiter on the Mona Capitolinus, where the Roman Senate met.

❑ Fierce fiery warriors fought upon the clouds,
In ranks and squadrons and right form of war,
Which drizzled blood upon the **Capitol**.—William Shakespeare

❐

carat / caret / carrot / karat

❏ A **carat** is the unit of weight for precious stones equal to 200 milligrams or about three grains.

❏ A **caret** is a wedge-shaped mark made on written or printed matter to indicate the place where something is to be inserted. On a keyboard it is the symbol ^ found above the numeral **6**.

❏ A **carrot** is a long pointed orange edible root. (By extension, it is something offered in order to encourage—the alternative to the stick.)

❏ A **karat is** a unit of fineness for gold equal to 1/24 part of pure gold in an alloy. 18-karat gold is 75% gold; 24-karat gold is pure gold

TANGENT: Triceratops & Carrots

How did English get four words that all sound alike, but are spelled differently and mean different things? It all has to do with how *triceratops* is related to *seeds* and *carrots*.

Caret is easy. It comes straight from the Latin *caret* ("it is lacking"). With ^ out of the way, we really have only two words left to deal with, *carrot* and *carat*. *Karat* is a variant of *carat* that's only been around since the beginning of the 20th century when U.S. jewelers started making the difference between the two. The British still use only the word *carat* for both gold and stones.

Carat comes from the Arabic *qirat*, a weight of four grains, which came from the Greek *kertion*, a weight equaling 1/3 of an *obol* (an *obol*, if you want to know, was 1/6 of a drachma). Originally a *kertion* was identical to the Roman *siliqua*; both were 1/24 of the golden *solidus* of Constantine, which was 1/6 of an ounce. That's why the various values wound up being in 1/24ths.

The Greek word *kertion* was a diminutive of the word for horn—*keras*—and meant "little horn, fruit of carob or locust tree." Carob trees are native to the Mediterranean region. The trees produce small, edible seedpods containing carob beans. (Most of us have come across these ground seeds. They are often used as substitute for cocoa.) The connection to weight comes from the nature of the carob beans: they are unusually consistent in size. Carob beans usually all weigh the same, no matter when or where harvested. This handy attribute led to carob beans becoming a weight standard in antiquity.

The word *carrot* has been used in English since at least 1533. It comes from the Middle French *carotte*, which came from the Late Latin *carota*, which came from the Greek *karOton*. Remember the Greek *keras* that meant horn? We also get words like *keratin* (a tough, insoluble protein

⇨

Tangent (continued)

substance that is the chief structural constituent of hair, nails, horns, and hooves), *rhinoceros* (Latin *rhinoceros* from Greek *rhinokeros* from Greek *rhs, rhn-*, nose + *keras*, horn), and *triceratops* (Greek *tri-*, three + Greek *keras*, horn + Greek *ops*, eye, face).

Keras is a descendent of the Indo-European root **ker-*. **Ker-* words usually have something to do with "animal's horn," but also include words for *top* and *head*. The root gives us many head- and horn-related words (including the word *horn* itself.) We could explain how *carrot* is closely related to *hornet*, but just as too little knowledge is dangerous, so, too, is too much knowledge.

❑

censer / censor / censure / sensor

A **censer** is a covered incense burner swung on chains during religious rituals.

❑ Then, methought, the air grew denser, perfumed from an unseen **censer** Swung by seraphim whose footfalls tinkled on the tufted floor.
—Edgar Allan Poe

A **censor** is one who supervises conduct and morals or an official who examines and suppresses that which is deemed objectionable.

❑ Satires which the **censor** understands are rightly prohibited.
—Karl Kraus

Censure is severe criticism and condemnation.

❑ **Censure** is the tax a man pays to the public for being eminent.
—Jonathan Swift

A **sensor** is a device that receives and responds to a signal or stimulus (such as heat, light, pressure, motion, etc.). *Sensor* can also mean "sense organ."

❑ Explorer I carried a **sensor** designed by Dr. James Van Allen that helped identify the radiation belts—now known as the Van Allen Belts—that ring the Earth.

❑

cents / scents / sense / since

Cents are monetary units.

❑ Hollywood is a place where they'll pay you a thousand dollars for a kiss and fifty **cents** for your soul.—Marilyn Monroe

Scents means "odors." As a verb it means "to smell" or "catch the meaning of something."

❑ One has a nose. The nose **scents** and it chooses. An artist is simply a kind of pig snouting truffles.—Igor Stravinsky

As a noun, **sense** has several meanings including "faculty of perception"; "consensus"; "an ability to reliably use intelligence"; "discerning awareness."

❑ If I had no **sense** of humor, I would long ago have committed suicide. —Mohandas Gandhi

Since means "position throughout" or "within period after"; "during" or "in time after"; "because"; "from that time or event until now."

❑ **Since** the day of my birth, my death began its walk. It is walking toward me, without hurrying.—Jean Cocteau

❐

cereal / serial

Cereal is breakfast food prepared from grain or the grass from which starchy edible grains (wheat, rice, rye, oats, maize, buckwheat, millet) are obtained.

❑ The idea that you can merchandise candidates for high office like breakfast **cereal**—that you can gather votes like box tops—is, I think, the ultimate indignity to the democratic process.—Adlai Stevenson

Serial means "arranged in a series; one after another."

❑ An autobiography is an obituary in **serial** form with the last installment missing.—Quentin Crisp.

TANGENT: To Be Continued

Movie **serials** in the United States began in 1912 as a device to boost circulation of a magazine, *McClure's Ladies World*. Each issue began featuring a story with a continuing heroine that coincided with a motion picture of her adventures. The film, *What Happened to Mary*, was produced by The Edison Company and was an instant hit. Soon other serials not associated with magazines appeared.

⇨

Tangent (continued)

Although the earliest serials did not have "cliffhanger" endings, episodes (ranging from twelve to fifteen per story) soon were designed to end with the protagonist in dire peril. It became imperative to return the following week, and the next, and so on—to see how it all turned out.

The Golden Age of movie serials is considered to be 1935–1940. They died out in 1956 when television became the prime dispenser of episodic adventure.

□

chord / cord

A **chord** is a combination of musical tones played simultaneously.

❑ One **chord** is fine. Two chords are pushing it. Three chords and you're into jazz.—Lou Reed

A **cord** is:

❍ A long slender flexible material usually consisting of several strands woven or twisted together.

❑ Or ever the silver **cord** be loosed, or the golden bowl be broken, or the pitcher be broken at the fountain, or the wheel broken at the cistern. —Ecclesiastes 12:6

❍ An emotional bond.

❑ The daughter's emotional **cord** to her mother snapped her back home.

❍ One of several anatomical structures resembling a cord.

❑ He who joyfully marches to music in rank and file has already earned my contempt. He has been given a large brain by mistake, since for him the spinal **cord** would suffice.—Albert Einstein

❍ A flexible insulated electrical cable.

❑ We need a 12-foot extension **cord** for the lamp.

❍ A unit of wood cut for fuel equal to a stack 4 x 4 x 8 feet or 128 cubic feet

❑ The wood in one **cord** would make 942 one pound books.

□

chute / shoot

A **chute** is an incline down which articles can slide. It is also a shortened version of *parachute*.

❏ Sliding down the Death Star's garbage **chute** seemed like a good idea until the sides began moving inward to compact the trash.

The most common meanings of **shoot** as a noun are "the act of discharging a weapon" and "new growth." Among the many verb meanings are "to hit with a missile" and "to send forth with force or swiftly."

❏ To talk without thinking is to **shoot** without aiming.—English proverb

❐

cite / sight / site

To **cite** is to quote.

❏ The devil can **cite** Scripture for his purpose.—William Shakespeare

Sight is vision.

❏ **Sight** and all the other senses are only modes of touch.—Samuel Butler

Site is an exact location

❏ He who overlooks a healthy spot for the **site** of his house is mad and ought to be handed over to the care of his relations and friends. —Marcus Terentius Varro

❐

coarse / course

Coarse is an adjective that means "rough."

❏ Tea, though ridiculed by those who are naturally **coarse** in their nervous sensibilities... will always be the favourite beverage of the intellectual. —Thomas De Quincey

Course is used as a noun or verb has many meanings. The most common meanings for the noun are:

❍ A mode of action.

❏ I know not what **course** others may take; but as for me, give me liberty, or give me death.—Patrick Henry

❍ Unit of study (or series of units of study).

❏ I took a speed-reading **course** and read *War and Peace* in twenty minutes. It involves Russia—Woody Allen

⇨

○ A line or route along which something travels or moves.

❑ Down on the plains, rivers run in their **course** as straightforward as time, channeled toward the sea.—Lynn Noel

○ General line of orientation.

❑ And it's a fair wind blowin' warm out of the south over my shoulder Guess I'll set a **course** and go.—David Crosby

○ A natural development; progress.

❑ When, in the **course** of human events, it becomes necessary for one people to dissolve the political bands which have connected them with another...—Thomas Jefferson

○ An area used for a sports event.

❑ The only time my prayers are never answered is on the golf **course**. —Billy Graham.

○ A continuous horizontal layer of bricks or other building material.

❑ The wall grew higher as each **course** of brick was added.

○ A part of a meal served one at a time.

❑ She was a woman who, between **courses**, could be graceful with her elbows on the table.—Henry James

The phrase meaning "the ordinary way or as might be expected" is **of course.**

❑ It is better, **of course,** to know useless things than to know nothing. —Tom Stoppard

⊓

complacence / complacent / complaisant / compliant

Complacence is a noun meaning "contented self-satisfied." **Complacent,** "contented to a fault," is an adjective.

❑ A **complacent** satisfaction with present knowledge is the chief bar to the pursuit of knowledge.—B.H. Liddell Hart

Complaisant means "eager to please, obliging."

❑ I'd hate to go through life without ever making anyone hot under the collar. It's important to irritate people who are religiously committed, **complaisant,** and smug in their ignorance.—Catherine Fahringer

Compliant means "willing to comply or obey, submissive."

❑ Too bad men aren't like computers: predictable, **compliant,** full of answers but no questions...yet able to deliver an occasional delightful surprise.—Brenda Starr

⊓

complement / compliment

These two spellings were once used interchangeably, but modern usage has defined a role for each.

Complement, as a noun, means "something that completes or brings to perfection."

❏ Anger and humor are like the left and right arm. They **complement** each other. Anger empowers the poor to declare their uncompromising opposition to oppression, and humor prevents them from being consumed by their fury.—James Cone

❏ Victory depended on using the full **complement** of weapons in their arsenal.

Complement, as a verb, means to "serve as a complement to."

❏ The bride's bouquet should **complement** her dress and body shape.

Compliment (noun) is an expression of praise or act of courtesy or praise.

❏ Rarely has a people paid the lavish **compliment** and taken the subtle revenge of turning its oppressor's speech into sorcery.—T.E. Kalem

Compliment, used as a verb, means "to pay a compliment to."

❏ Whenever a man's friends begin to **compliment** him about looking young, he may be sure that they think he is growing old.—Victor Hugo

❐

conscience / conscious

Conscience is an inner sense of right and wrong.

❏ **Conscience** is God present in man.—Victor Hugo

Conscious means "aware" or "awake."

❏ The mind that's **conscious** of its rectitude laughs at the lies of rumor. —Ovid

❐

consul / council / counsel

A **consul** is an official appointed by a government to reside in a foreign country to represent the interests of the appointing country.

❑ The first Siamese cat in America was a gift from the American **consul** in Bangkok to Lucy Webb Hayes, wife of President Rutherford B. Hayes.

A **council** is an elected or appointed group of people assembled for governing or advising.

❑ You can't expect me to wear blue jeans to the Security **Council**.
—Nora Astorga, UN delegate, Nicaragua

Counsel means

○ To give advice or opinion (verb) as in *Volunteers* **counsel** *the young people.*

○ The advice or opinion itself (noun).

❑ Evil **counsel** travels fast.—Sophocles

○ A legal advisor (noun) as in *On advice of* **counsel**, *he refused to testify.*

❏

corps / corpse

A **corps** *(kor)* is a military unit or a group of associated persons (especially if they share a common activity or occupation).

❑ Literature takes shape and life in the body, in the wombs of the mother tongue: always: and the Fathers of Culture get anxious about paternity. They start talking about legitimacy. They steal the baby. They ensure by every means that the artist, the writer, is male. This involves intellectual abortion by centuries of women artists, infanticide of works by women writers, and a whole medical **corps** of sterilizing critics working to purify the Canon, to reduce the subject matter and style of literature to something Ernest Hemingway could have understood.
—Ursula K. Le Guin

A **corpse** *(korps)* is a dead body.

❑ When childhood dies, its **corpses** are called adults.—Brian W. Aldiss

❏

corespondents / correspondence / correspondents

Corespondents are joint defendants in a court case.

❑ Anna Held filed for divorce from Florenz Ziegfeld in 1912, naming Lilliane Lorraine as one of several **corespondents.**

Correspondence is communication (usually via letter).

❑ It seems a long time since the morning mail could be called **correspondence.**—Jacques Barzun

Correspondents are

○ Those with whom letters are exchanged.

❑ How dare I read Washington's campaigns, when I have not answered the letters of my own **correspondents**?—Ralph Waldo Emerson

○ Persons who report for the press often on a specific area.

❑ Those 40 or 50 national **correspondents** who had followed [John F.] Kennedy since the beginning of his electoral exertions into the November days had become more than a press corps-they had become his friends and, some of them, his most devoted admirers. —Theodore H. White

credible / creditable / credulous

Credible means "believable."

❑ Now we have a problem in making our power **credible**, and Viet Nam is the place.—John Fitzgerald Kennedy

Creditable means "deserving of praise or acknowledgement."

❑ Among the lighter sopranos Meta Seinemeyer gave some very creditable performances, improving as the season went on.... —*New York Tribune,* 1 April 1923

Credulous is an adjective that means "gullible".

❑ The most positive men are the most **credulous**.—Jonathan Swift

cue / queue

A **cue** is:

○ Anything done or said that is a signal to do something.

❑ Were it my **cue** to fight, I should have known it
Without a prompter.—William Shakespeare

○ A long stick used by pool and billiards players to hit the ball.

❑ He stood in the dimly lit barroom with a pool **cue** in one hand and a
beer in the other.

A **queue** is

○ A line of people or vehicles waiting for something.

❑ The **queue** for concert tickets was a block long.

○ A braid of hair at the back of the head.

❑ The Manchu emperors compelled all Chinese males to shave the front
of their heads and wear their hair in a single plait, or **queue**.

❐

currant /current

A **currant** is a type of tart red or black berry used primarily for jellies and jams.

❑ The black **currant** is the traditional source of the French liqueur, Cassis.

Current means:

○ Of the present time.

❑ **Current** illusion is that science has abolished all natural laws.
—Marshall McLuhan

○ A movement of water, air or electricity, in a particular direction.

❑ In matters of principals, stand like a rock; in matters of taste, swim with
the **current**.—Thomas Jefferson

❐

❧D❧

defuse / diffuse

Defuse means "to remove a triggering device or, by extension, to lessen the danger or tension."

❑ Enter no conflict against fanatics unless you can **defuse** them.
   —Frank Herbert

Diffuse means (verb) "to spread over a wide area or many directions"; as an adverb it acquires an additional meaning of "not clear, not easily understood, lacking conciseness."

❑ Aromatic plants bestow no spicy fragrance while they grow; but crush'd or trodden to the ground, **diffuse** their balmy sweets around.
   —Oliver Goldsmith

❐

desert / dessert

The noun **desert** (*DEZuhrt*) means "arid land or an empty or forsaken place."

❑ The task of the modern educator is not to cut down jungles, but to irrigate **deserts**.—C.S. Lewis

As an adjective, **desert** (*DEZuhrt*) relates to, is characteristic of, or inhabits a desert.

❑ Sotol is a **desert** shrub from which a powerful spirit is brewed.

It also means "barren and uninhabited; desolate."

❑ Three people marooned on a **desert** island would soon reinvent politics.—Mason Cooley

In its verb form, **desert** (*diZUHRT*) means to abandon or leave behind.

❑ She had been known to **desert** her post.

A **dessert** (*diZUHRT*) is a sweet course or dish served at the end of a meal

❑ Work is the meat of life, pleasure the **dessert**.—B.C. Forbes

⇨

The word *desert*—when spelled like "arid land" but pronounced like "sweet to end meal"—also refers to a deserved reward or punishment. In his *Sonnet 72,* Shakespeare says, "Unless you would devise some virtuous lie,/To do more for me than mine own desert." He is using the word *desert* to mean "worthiness; deserving." Someone who does wrong and is punished in a suitable manner has received his "just deserts."

❐

decent / descent / dissent

Decent *(DEE sent)* means "fitting, appropriate or in good taste."

❑ Every **decent** man is ashamed of the government he lives under.
—H.L. Mencken

Descent *(d SENT)* means (as a noun):

○ a decline or the act of moving downward.

❑ The **descent** to the infernal regions is easy enough, but to retrace one's steps, and reach the air above, there's the rub.—Virgil

○ Kinship between one and one's progenitors

❑ Genealogy, n. An account of one's **descent** from a man who did not particularly care to trace his own.—Ambroise Bierce

Dissent *(d SENT)* as a noun means "an opposition or disagreement; as a verb it means "to disagree or to differ in opinion."

❑ Here in America we are descended in blood and in spirit from revolutionists and rebels—men and women who dare to **dissent** from accepted doctrine. As their heirs, may we never confuse honest **dissent** with disloyal subversion.—Dwight D. Eisenhower

❐

dent / dint

You already know a **dent** is "a depression in a surface made by pressure or a blow." As a verb it means "to make or put a *dent* in." But if you look **dint** up in a dictionary, you may be surprised to find that *dint* can mean "dent." In the real world, *dint* retains only the meaning "force or effort" and is used primarily in the phrase *by dint of* which means "by force of."

❑ By **dint** of dogged charisma, [Yul] Brynner has identified himself with a role [in *The King and I*] more than any other actor since Bela Lugosi hung up his fangs.—Richard Corliss

❑ Let's make a **dent** in the universe.—Steve Jobs

❐

dew / do / due

Dew is moisture.

- ❑ Human life is like morning **dew**.—Chinese proverb

Do means "make, cause, perform, carry out, act," etc.

- ❑ You must **do** the things you think you can not **do**.—Eleanor Roosevelt

Due can mean (noun) "that which is owed or deserved" as in *The rent comes due at the end of the month.*

As an adjective **due** can mean "expected at a particular time" as in *Their first baby is due in two months.*

It can also mean "resulting" (as in *The accident was due to human error)* and, as an adverb, "straight" (as in *Head due west on Main Street*).

❒

die / dye

Die means:

- ○ To stop living or existing.
  - ❑ Men **die** in despair, while spirits **die** in ecstasy.—Honoré de Balzac
- ○ Device for shaping.
  - ❑ They designed a stamping **die** for a sheet metal automobile part.

Dye means "to color" (verb) or "the substance used to color" (noun).

- ❑ I had a lot of dates but I decided to stay home and **dye** my eyebrows. —Andy Warhol

The **-ing** forms of the two words can also be confusing. If you **dye** something you are **dyeing**. If you are coming to the end of your life you are **dying**.

❒

discreet / discrete

Discreet means "prudent, circumspect."

- ❑ Satire's my weapon, but I'm too **discreet**
  To run amuck, and tilt at all I meet.—Alexander Pope

Discrete means "separate, distinct."

- ❑ The writing course was divided into four **discrete** modules.

Tip: Keep them straight by remembering the *t* in **discrete** *separates* the two *e*'s.

❒

done / dun

Done is the past participle of *do*. (See above.)

❑ Well begun is half **done**.—Aristotle

Dun means:

○ to demand repeatedly

❑ Must we **dun** him in order to receive payment?

○ a dull grayish brown

❑ Earth wears a **dun**-colored dress
like an old woman wooing the sun to be her lover...
—Margaret Abigail Walker

❐

draft / draught / draughts

In North American and Australian English the word **draft** is used for all senses: to conscript for military service, a preliminary version, a money order drawn from a bank, a current of air, a quick gulp of liquid, beer or other beverage stored and served from a large container, depth of water needed to float ship, a dose of liquid, pulling a heavy load, etc.

❑ A corner **draft** fluttered the flame, and the white fever of temptation, upswept its angel wings that cast, a cruciform shadow.
—Boris Pasternak

❑ The **draft** is white people sending black people to fight yellow people to protect the country they stole from red people.—James Rado

In British English the word **draught** is used for a current of air, a quick gulp of liquid, beer or other beverage stored and served from a large container, depth of water needed to float ship, a dose of liquid, pulling a heavy load; the alternate spelling, **draft**, is used for the other meanings.

❑ O, for a **draught** of vintage! that hath been
Cooled a long age in the deep-delvid earth...—John Keats

Draughts is a board game similar to checkers (the object is to jump over and capture the opponent's pieces) for two players who each have 12 pieces.

❐

drier / dryer

A **drier** is someone or something that *dries*, including a substance put into paint to make it dry faster. It also means "more dry." A device or appliance used for drying clothes, hair, hands, boots, etc. is usually a **dryer**. A hair *dryer* makes your hair *drier*. These uses are, however, not solidly established.

- ❏ The valley we call Death, isn't really that different from much of the rest of the desert West. It's just a little deeper, a little hotter and a little **drier**. What sets it apart more than anything else is the mind's eye. —Richard E. Lingenfelter

- ❏ Nowadays, they have more trouble packing hair **dryers** than baseball equipment.—Bob Feller

dual / duel

Dual means "double."

- ❏ The love between man and woman is the greatest and most complete passion the world will ever see, because it is **dual**, because it is of two opposing kinds.—D.H. Lawrence

A **duel** is a fight between two.

- ❏ In the **duel** of sex woman fights from a dreadnought and man from an open raft.—H.L. Mencken

duck tape / duct tape

Despite what you may read in your dictionary, **duct tape** really did start out being called **duck tape**. The adhesive was created in 1942 for the U.S. military to keep dampness out of ammunition cases. The olive drab tape was dubbed *duck tape* because it was waterproof and made from cotton duck fabric. Many uses other than taping ammo cases were quickly discovered and *duck tape* definitely did its bit to win WW2.

After the war, the tape went to work joining heating and air conditioning ductwork. The military green became a dull silver to match the ducts. That's when folks starting calling it *duct tape*. In 1984, Manco Inc. registered "Duck Tape" as a trademark for its *duct tape*.

Even though *duck* appears to be as correct as *duct* for the sticky stuff (which is no longer recommended for sealing ducts) the standard term is *duct tape*.

- ❏ **Duct tape** is like the Force. It has a light side and a dark side and it holds the universe together.—Carl Zwanzi

E

egoism / egotism

Egoism is the less common and more technical word for an ethical theory that treats self-interest as the foundation of morality.

❑ No **egoism** is so insufferable as that of the Christian with regard to his soul.—W. Somerset Maugham

Egotism means "excessive conceit or self-absorption."

❑ **Egotism** is the anesthetic that dulls the pain of stupidity.—Frank Leahy

❐

e.g. / i.e.

These two Latin abbreviations are not interchangeable: **i.e.** stands for *id est,* and means "that is"; **e.g.** stands for *exempli gratia,* meaning "for example." In American English usage, both are followed by a comma after the second period. This is not so in British English. American usage calls for periods after each letter and no spaces. In British English, **eg** and **ie** are often written with no periods. (Yanks are always over-punctuating, aren't they?)

You should not use *etc.* with *e.g.* By using *e.g.* you are telling the reader you are providing a few examples, not a complete list. Using *etc.* at the end of such a list is, therefore, redundant.

In most writing, it's probably best to avoid the Latin and use English, but see the *Tangent* on page 153 for more Latin abbreviations.

❐

elicit / illicit

Elicit means "to draw out."

❑ Act so as to **elicit** the best in others and thereby in thyself.—Felix Adler

Illicit means "not allowed or unlawful."

❑ Never seek **illicit** wealth.—Confucius

❐

elusive / illusive

Elusive means "hard to catch or grasp."

❑ In the attitude of silence the soul finds the path in a clearer light, and what is **elusive** and deceptive resolves itself into crystal clearness. Our life is a long and arduous quest after Truth.—Mahatma Gandhi

Illusive means "deceptive or unreal."

❑ It's been **illusive** for so long, but freedom is mine today.—India.arie

emerge / immerge

Emerge means "to come out of something enclosed."

❑ Innumerable confusions and a feeling of despair invariably **emerge** in periods of great technological and cultural transition.
—Marshall McLuhan

Immerge means "to submerge or disappear in or as if in a liquid." (The synonym *immerse* is much more commonly used.)

❑ Their souls are **immerged** in matter.—Jeremy Taylor

emigration / immigration

Emigration is moving *from* a country.

❑ **Emigration**, forced or chosen, across national frontiers or from village to metropolis, is the quintessential experience of our time.—John Berger

Immigration is moving *to* a country.

❑ No matter what other nations may say about the United States, **immigration** is still the sincerest form of flattery.—Clayton Cramer

eminent / imminent

Eminent means "outstanding, revered."

❑ Life levels all men. Death reveals the **eminent**.—George Bernard Shaw

Imminent means "threatening to happen soon."

❑ Noble life demands a noble architecture for noble uses of noble men. Lack of culture means what it has always meant: ignoble civilization and therefore **imminent** downfall.—Frank Lloyd Wright

enclose / inclose (also *enclosure / inclosure*)

Although once used interchangeably, American dictionaries and editors now seem to prefer **enclose** and the *OED* definitely prefers **enclose.**

❑ Your pain is the breaking of the shell that **encloses** your understanding. —Kahlil Gibran

◻

enquire / inquire (also *enquirer / enquiry; inquirer / inquiry*)

In the U.S., only **inquire** is used. In Australia and the U.K a distinction is sometimes still made: **enquire** means "to ask in general," while **inquire** means "to make a formal investigation." The police or an official commission would *inquire.*

❑ My advice to you is not to **inquire** why or whither, but just enjoy your ice cream while it's on your plate.—Thornton Wilder

◻

envelop / envelope

Envelop means "to wrap up, cover, or completely surround."

❑ Accompanying the darkness, a stillness **envelops** the city.—Curtis Wilkie

An **envelope** is a paper container used to enclose a letter or document.

❑ Letters are expectation packaged in an **envelope.**—Shana Alexander

◻

every day / everyday

Every day (two words) is each day.

❑ Read, **every day**, something no one else is reading. Think, **every day**, something no one else is thinking. Do, **every day**, something no one else would be silly enough to do. It is bad for the mind to continually be part of unanimity.—Christopher Morley

Everyday is ordinary routine, the commonplace.

❑ The whole of science is nothing more than a refinement of **everyday** thinking.—Albert Einstein

◻

every one / everyone

Every one (two words) means "each person individually."

❑ Dreaming permits each and **every one** of us to be quietly and safely insane every night of our lives.—William Dement

Everyone refers to all members of a group.

❑ Let **everyone** sweep in front of his own door, and the whole world will be clean.—Johann Wolfgang von Goethe

◗

exceptionable / exceptional

Exceptionable means "something one might take exception to; objectionable, debatable."

❑ Bishop Hurd undertook his well-known edition, in which the most **exceptionable** Poetry (that had operated like a mill-stone and sunk the rest) is omitted, and the generality of his charms preserved, [and] has now a dozen readers where before he had scarce one.—Henry Headley

Exceptional means "uncommon, outstanding, extraordinary."

❑ The thing that makes you **exceptional**, if you are at all, is inevitably that which must also make you lonely.—Lorraine Hansberry

◗

explicit / implicit

Explicit means "stated outright, fully and clearly expressed."

❑ What is grand is necessarily obscure to weak men. That which can be made **explicit** to the idiot is not worth my care.—William Blake

Implicit means "implied, understood though not directly expressed."

❑ Once the **implicit** aim of biography was to uplift… now it is to unveil.—Mark Feeney

◗

F

faint / feint

The noun **faint** means "a temporary loss of consciousness." As a verb it means "to lose consciousness."

❑ Oh, lift me from the grass!
I die! I **faint**! I fail!
Let thy love in kisses rain
On my lips and eyelids pale.—Percy Bysshe Shelley

As an adjective **faint** can mean "feeble or timid."

❑ **Faint** heart never won fair lady.—Miguel de Cervantes

The adjective **faint** also can mean "lacking brightness, clarity, or distinctness."

❑ The gap between the committed and the indifferent is a Sahara whose **faint** trails, followed by the mind's eye only, fade out in sand.
—Nadine Gordimer

A **feint** is a misleading attack.

❑ The boxer made a **feint** to the left and followed it with a right jab.

❏

fair / fare

Fair can mean:

◯ Exhibition or marketplace.

❑ The farmers crowd to the **fair** today in obedience to the same ancient law,... as naturally as bees swarm and follow their queen.
—Henry David Thoreau

◯ Moderately good but less than excellent, average.

❑ Miss [Margaret] Truman is a unique American phenomenon with a pleasant voice of little size and **fair** quality. There are few moments during her recital when one can relax and feel confident that she will make her goal, which is the end of the song.—Paul Hume

⇨

○ Good, but not excessive or extreme.

❑ Every man should keep a **fair**-sized cemetery in which to bury the faults of his friends.—Henry Ward Beecher

○ Pleasing to the eye.

❑ A **fair** lady's smile is worth more than a thousand ounces of gold.—Chinese proverb

○ Free from clouds; pleasant weather.

❑ So foul and **fair** a day I have not seen.—William Shakespeare

○ Just.

❑ Life isn't **fair**. It's just **fairer** than death, that's all.—William Goldman

○ Conforming with established standards.

❑ **Fair** use is important to innovators as well as consumers. It's **fair** use that allowed the VCR to innovate on top of the television.—Joe Krauss

○ Pale or light-colored.

❑ His **fair** hair, so **fair** and golden as to be almost effeminate, clustered over his white forehead, which was high and well-formed. —Victor Hugo

Fare can mean:

○ Cost of a ride in a vehicle.

❑ Conductor, when you receive a **fare**,
Punch in the presence of the passenjare:
A blue trip slip for an eight-cent **fare**,
A buff trip slip for a six-cent **fare**,
A pink trip slip for a three-cent **fare**,
Punch in the presence of the passenjare!—Mark Twain

○ Experience good or bad results.

❑ Fortune raises up and fortune brings low both the man who **fares** well and the one who **fares** badly; and there is no prophet of the future for mortal men.—Sophocles

○ Something offered for consumption, such as food, drink, or entertainment.

❑ Cassoulet, that best of bean feasts, is everyday **fare** for a peasant but ambrosia for a gastronome...—Julia Child

❐

farther / further

> **Son** (Zeppo Marx): Anything further, Father?
> **Father** (Groucho Marx): "Anything further, Father?" That can't be right. Isn't it "anything farther, further?"
> —S.J. Perelman, screenwriter, *Horsefeathers*

Farther means "more distant in space; actual or literal distance."

❑ California is where you can't run any **farther** without getting wet.
—Neil Morgan

Further means "additional or more."

❑ The **further** through life I drift
The more obvious it becomes that
I am lacking in thrift.—Ogden Nash

❑

faun / fawn

These days, **faun** is used to connote a gentler version of the more lustful satyr—woodland demi-gods with goatlike-horns and ears who resemble goats from the waist down. (Want more mythological information? See the *Tangent* below.)

❑ Everything began with images; a **faun** carrying an umbrella, a queen on a sledge, a magnificent lion.—C.S. Lewis

A **fawn** is a young deer or a light grayish yellowish brown color.

❑ *Bambi: A Life in the Woods* by Felix Salten is the story of a **fawn** and his adventures as he grows into a young buck.

❑ Siamese cats have almond-shaped blue eyes, and white, cream, or **fawn**-colored coats with brown or gray feet, tail, ears, and face.

TANGENT: Piper at the Gates of Fawn?*

Okay, we have a goatish forest dude, a baby deer, and a color similar to the deer's color. Which one do you use when you mean *to try to gain favor by flattery, over praising, and paying a lot of (probably insincere) attention* (colloquially know as "majorly sucking-up")? That's **fawn**, as in "The media **fawns** over celebrities."

What does flattery have to do with baby deer? Nothing. The deer-type word *fawn* comes the Latin root *foetus* meaning "offspring" (from whence the word "fetus" also comes). The *fawn* involving obsequious behavior comes from the Old English *fagnian*, "to rejoice." Since *fawn* also means "to show delight or fondness (by wagging the tail, whining, etc.) as a dog does," you can see the connection: just picture a dog rejoicing over a master's attention. ⇨

Tangent (Continued)

Promised Mythological Note: Faunus was a rustic Roman god with the power of prophecy and influence over the fertility of crops and flocks. He spoke to his followers through the sounds of the forest and in nightmares. Faunus came to be regarded as an early king of Latium who taught his people agriculture.

The later urbanized Romans associated Faunus and his attendant creatures, fauns, with the Greek god Pan and the Dionysiac satyrs. In earlier images Faunus had the ears and legs of a horse. With the Romans he gained Pan's attributes of goat's legs, but retained his horse's ears. Ovid identified Faunus as the god of the Lupercalia [15 February].

Faunus' wife, daughter, or sister (or perhaps all three) was Fauna, a goddess of chastity, fertility, and healing. Fauna was also identified with the Bona Dea (a title meaning "good goddess"), whose worship was restricted exclusively to women. Fauna and Faunus were both linked to prophecies spoken in ecstatic or intoxicated states.

In the late 18th century, *fauna* began to be used to mean animal life of a particular region or epoch. *Flora*, from the name of the Roman goddess of flowers, was adopted to mean plant life in the same context.

—ᴍ—

* "Piper at the Gates of *Dawn*" was the title of Chapter Seven of the children's classic *The Wind in the Willows* by Kenneth Grahame. It was used as the title of Pink Floyd's debut album (August 1967.)

---

faze / phase

To **faze** is to disconcert, upset the composure.

❑ The boisterous crowd did not **faze** the pitcher.

A **phase** is an aspect or stage of development.

❑ The East is marvellously interesting for tracing our steps back. But for going forward, it is nothing. All it can hope for is to be fertilised by Europe, so that it can start on a new **phase**.
—D.H. Lawrence

TANGENT: Set Phaser On Stun

The **phaser** was the weapon of choice for the crew of the starship Enterprise. Gene Roddenberry supposedly called his fictional creation a "phaser" instead of "laser" or "laser-gun" so viewers would not be troubled by thoughts of whether or not lasers could actually perform as they did in the *Star Trek* scripts. Encounters with a phaser, however, certainly **fazed** many—at least fictionally.

---

feat / feet / fete / fête

A **feat** is noteworthy deed.

❏ Nature arms each man with some faculty which enables him to do easily some **feat** impossible to any other, and thus makes him necessary to society.—Ralph Waldo Emerson

Feet is the plural of foot.

❏ A man's **feet** must be planted in his country, but his eyes should survey the world.—George Santayana

❏ Ice doesn't freeze three **feet** thick over night.—Chinese proverb

A **fete** (pronounced to rhyme with either *mate* or *met*) is a festival or feast. It can also mean "an elaborate party." **Fête** is the same word as *fete* and it inspires a *Tangent* on diacritical marks.

TANGENT: Diacritical Marks Critique

Once a word is adopted into English from another language, it often loses diacritical marks like the little rooftop over the *e* (more properly known as a circumflex) in *fête*. At least it does in American English. British English retains more of the original orthography. The *Chicago Manual of Style* leaves decisions concerning diacritics to the dictionary (*Webster's* latest edition, in their case). Another style standard is to abandon the accents with words that have become completely anglicized. Some of those are fairly easy to determine. Words like *critique, regime, role, suede,* and *premiere* are rarely seen with marks. Others, like *appliqué, auto-da-fé, façade, doppelgänger,* and *tête-à-tête,* are "iffy." Still others are probably more "foreign" than "English": *outré, piñata, touché, exposé, déjà vu.* Dictionaries often disagree on which is which.

Computers now make it much easier to use orthographics. (Plain text e-mail poses a special problem, though, because of the way many American servers process characters.) It's still difficult for deadline-oriented news media to use them consistently and correctly, so they often drop all diacritics. Some break their own rules when it comes to proper names (like Björk). Some don't.

We have no single solution. We skip orthographics ourselves when using ASCII (text only), but in anything formatted we tend to side with the Brits and use the accent (acute and grave), cidilla, circumflex, dieresis or umlaut, and tilde unless a word is definitely "englished." We do not use the breve, double acute accent, macron, ogonek, or caron. We have been known to use a háček occasionally, but then we know what *"Prepáčte, nerozumiem"* means. (Although we can't pronounce it.)

❐

fewer / less

Use **fewer** for things you count (individually).

❑ The **fewer** men, the greater share of honor.—William Shakespeare

Use **less** for things you measure. Less refers to amount or degree as distinct from a series of individual items.

❑ I either want **less** corruption, or more chance to participate in it. —Ashleigh Brilliant

❐

fir / fur

A **fir** is a type of evergreen tree.

❑ The slender **fir** that taper grows, The sturdy oak with broad-spread boughs.—John Dyer

Fur is animal hair.

❑ Many bits of fox **fur** will make a fine robe.—Chinese proverb

❐

flair/ flare

Flair is a natural ability to do something well.

❑ Short-term amnesia is not the worst affliction if you have an Irish **flair** for the sauce.—Norman Mailer

One meaning of **flare** is "flame up with a bright, wavering light."

❑ Life moves out of a red **flare** of dreams Into a common light of common hours, Until old age bring the red **flare** again. —William Butler Yeats

A flare can also be a signaling device using bright light *(The police left flares burning by the accident site.)* OR outward spread *(The actor's nostrils flare as he rolls his eyes.),* OR to erupt or intensify suddenly. *(Her fever flares up from time to time. Tempers flared but cooler heads soon prevailed.)*

❐

floe / flow

A **floe** is a large sheet of floating ice.

❑ Eliza leaped from one ice **floe** to another with desperate energy .

Flow means "to move, run freely, circulate."

❑ A **flow** of words is a sure sign of duplicity.—Honoré de Balzac

❐

flew / flu / flue

Flew is the past tense of *fly*.

❑ Out **flew** the web and floated wide;
The mirror cracked from side to side;...—Alfred Tennyson

Flu is a shortened term for "influenza."

❑ In 1919, all over a Europe filled with graves, hung miasmas and miseries, and over the whole world too, because of the **flu** and its nearly thirty million deaths.—Doris Lessing

A **flue** is a passage to let air or gas escape

❑ If you discover Chimney Swifts in your **flue**, you may have to wait until after nesting season to remove the birds because they are protected under the Migratory Bird Treaty of 1918.

❐

flier / flyer

The Brits don't bother with the *i* version. It's **flyer** for *aviator* (or anything that flies) or *handbill* and that's that. Most American usage experts don't bother with the *y* version and prefer **flier** for both. The *Associated Press Stylebook* prefers **flier** for both, but allows that **Flyer** is the proper name of some trains, buses, sports teams, and the red wagon. *Words Into Type* does not take the issue up, but uses **flyers** for the riders (notes) attached to a manuscript. We have seen publications that specify using **flyer** for *handbill* and **flier** for *aviator*. Some dictionaries say **flier** and **flyer** can be used interchangeably.

What should you do? Unless you are writing for a publication with an established style, pick a method and use consistently or call pilots *pilots*, airplane passengers *airplane passengers*, birds *birds*, etc. and use *handbill, pamphlet, circular*, etc. for the other.

What about those "points" that accrue with airlines that can be exchanged for upgrades, travel, etc.? A Google search for "frequent flier" found 61,200 entries; "frequent flyer" resulted in 289,000.

❐

flounder / founder

Most of us know that **founder** means one who establishes something (as in *Clara Barton was the founder of the American Red Cross*) and know a **flounder** is a fish. It's when we come to the **verbs,** *founder* and *flounder,* that we get confused.

To **flounder** is to thrash about or to proceed in confusion.

- ❑ Guilt or innocence becomes irrelevant in the criminal trials as we **flounder** in a morass of artificial rules poorly conceived and often impossible [to apply].—Warren E. Burger

Founder means "to collapse or fail completely; to sink."

- ❑ Lastly, his tomb shall list and **founder** in the troughs of grass
  And none shall speak his name—Karl Shapiro

for / fore / four

For is a preposition meaning "on account or because of."

- ❑ Ask not what your country can do **for** you; ask what you can do **for** your country.—John F. Kennedy

Fore means "at or to the front."

- ❑ True human goodness, in all its purity and freedom, can come to the **fore** only when its recipient has no power.—Milan Kundera

Four is a number one more than three.

- ❑ Three Spaniards, **four** opinions.—Spanish proverb

The warning cry in golf is **fore**, probably a contraction of **before**. Its first use in this context was recorded in 1878.

forbear / forebear

Forbear means "to abstain or refrain from."

- ❑ If pleasure was not followed by pain, who would **forbear** it?
  —Samuel Johnson

A **forebear** is an ancestor or precursor.

- ❑ John Polidori's aristocratic vampire, Lord Ruthven, is Count Dracula's literary **forebear**.

forego (foregoing, foregone) / forgo (forgoing)

The **easy** explanation:

> *Forgo* means "refrain." *Forego*, which is relatively rare, means "precede." Thus, *foregone conclusion*, an outcome determined *before*hand. [from Kenneth Grahame's *The New York Times Manual of Style and Usage* (1999)]

Stick with the above and you'll be right, but if you are correcting others using *forego* to mean "to abstain," you might need further explanation. (English usage is a volatile issue in some circles. Please note we avoid any responsibility in this case by citing established authorities.)

The American Heritage Book of English Usage (1999) sums up the situation:

> If you are *foregoing* dessert, does that mean you are entering the dining room before it is brought in? The trouble here is that there are two *foregos*. The verb *forgo*—without the *e*—means "to do without" but has as an acceptable variant the spelling *forego*. Thus you can legitimately *forgo* or *forego* dessert. The other *forego* means "to go before, either in place or time," as in *A bad reputation often foregoes you*. This *forego* always has an *e*.

Kenneth G. Wilson, in *The Columbia Guide to Standard American English* (1993):

> The infrequent and stiffly Formal *forego* means "to go before, to precede," as in *The ceremony will forego the reception*. *Forgo* means "to abstain, to neglect, to overlook" as in *We'll forgo meeting until next week*. *Forego* is also an occasional variant spelling of *forgo*, but it's better to avoid it and the unnecessary confusion it can cause.

❒

foreword / forward

A **foreword** is a brief and simple introduction in a book.

❑ England has the most sordid literary scene I've ever seen. They all meet in the same pub. This guy's writing a **foreword** for this person....They're all scratching each other's backs.—William Burroughs

Forward means "onward" or "toward the front."

❑ Youth looks **forward** but age looks back.—British proverb

❒

formally/ formerly

Formally means "to be done in a formal manner." (*Formal* means "in accordance with rules, convention; ceremonial, solemn; relating to the external rather than substance; reserved or aloof.")

❑ Martin Luther was **formally** excommunicated in 1520.

Formerly means "previously."

❑ There is now less flogging in our great schools than **formerly**, but then less is learned there; so that what the boys get at one end they lose at the other.—Samuel Johnson

❑

forth / fourth

Forth means "forward."

❑ Behold, I send you **forth** as sheep in the midst of wolves: be ye therefore wise as serpents, and harmless as doves.—Matthew 10:16

Fourth comes after "third" and before "fifth."

❑ Character consists of what you do on the third and **fourth** tries. —James A. Michener

❑

foul / fowl

Foul means:

○ Offensive, extremely unpleasant, dirty.

❑ Grim death, how **foul** and loathsome is thine image. —William Shakespeare

○ To pollute something or make it dirty.

❑ Every day in Mexico City's Federal District more than 350 tons of waste from 2 million dogs dries into dust that combines with erosion, factory particles, and hydrocarbons from car exhausts to **foul** the air.

○ An act that is against the rules of a sport.

❑ Fans still ruin expensive suits going after **foul** balls that cost five dollars. Hitting streaks still make the network news and hot dogs still taste better at the ballpark than at home.—Duke Snider

A **fowl** is a bird, especially that of a type used to produce meat or eggs

❑ To-night she will spread her brown hair on his pillow, But I shall be hearing the harsh cries of wild **fowl**.—Patrick MacDonogh

❑

❧G❧

gamut / gantlet / gauntlet

Gamut means "the full range" and was originally applied to the medieval musical scale. Now it is a range (literally or figuratively) of anything. *(His feelings ran the gamut from delight to disgust.)* The phrase *run the gamut* is a common one, but it is sometimes confused with another phrase, *run the gantlet*.

A **gantlet** is an ordeal in which the offender runs between two lines of punishers who beat him or her with sticks or other implements. (Nowadays the *gantlets* we run are usually figurative.) *Gantlet* is often confused with **gauntlet**. (And, as we shall soon see, for damned good reason.)

Gauntlet originally referred to a glove worn as part of medieval armor. *Throwing down the gauntlet* issues a challenge. *Taking up the gauntlet* means accepting the challenge.

As far as American usage (British English does not use *gantlet*) you could just leave it there. Word maven William Safire says *gantlet* means "a course of discipline that you run past guys with clubs whacking at you from both sides." The *New York Times* and the Associated Press agree.

But to be honest, some American authorities say both words can be spelled *gauntlet* and have *gantlet* as a variant. *Run the gauntlet* has been commonly used more frequently than *run the gantlet*.

The mother of all dictionaries, the *Oxford English Dictionary*, is British, so it doesn't even recognize *gantlet* as anything but a variant of gauntlet. *Merriam-Webster*, an American standard, agrees with the *OED*. Canadian Press style, unlike Associated Press, does not allow *gantlet*, but the *Montreal Gazette* sanctions *gantlet* ["two lines of shtarkers who flog you as you pass through (or, figuratively, an ordeal); a *gauntlet* is a glove."]

The Australians are probably off at the pub sinking a pint at this point—or maybe that's drinking a schooner—and perhaps it would be wise to join them. But we do have one more item to cover: railroads.

According to *The American Heritage Book of English Usage* (1996) *gantlet* (as in the punishment) also became a railroad term (at least in the U.S.) for a section of track designed so that one rail of each track is inside the rails of the other. This allows trains on separate tracks to pass through a very narrow space. Discussion with railroaders, however, will also turn up the spelling *gauntlet* as acceptable.

❑

gibe / gybe / jibe / jive

In Associated Press style **gibe** means "to taunt or sneer." (*Fans often gibe at the kicker if he misses a field goal.*) It can also be used as a noun for such a comment. (*Each gibe was another painful wound to her pride.*) **Jibe,** according to AP, has two meanings. One, which they consider colloquial, means "to agree." (When *jibe* is used in this sense it is often used negatively, as in *these numbers don't jibe* or *the suspect's alibi does not jibe with the evidence.*) The other, "to shift direction," is derived from a third meaning for *jibe* used in sailing: "a change of tack while going downwind." (More or less—sailing jargon is not our forte.)

Most American dictionaries prefer *gibe* for the "scoff, taunt" sense with *jibe* considered a "variant." *Jibe* is preferred for both the nautical and "agree" meanings.

Jibe, however, is preferred in U.K. dictionaries with *gibe* mentioned as "American" or a variant. **Gybe** seems to be the preferred Brit sailing term with *jibe* as an alternative. Although we found instances of *gibe* used by both *The Times* of London and the BBC, the U.K. *Guardian* style guide uses *jibe* not *gibe.*

The "insulting, mocking" *jibe/gibe* (according to the *OED*) probably came into English in the 16th century from the Middle French *giber* ("to handle roughly"). The Dutch word *gijben,* meaning "the boom or spar of a sailing ship," is the source for *jibe/gybe. Jibe* meaning "to agree" did not enter until the early 19th century. The best the *OED* can do with it etymologically is to suggest it may be "phonetically related" to *chime* (as in the phrase *chime in*).

The word **jive** is often very mistakenly used to mean **jibe,** as in "these numbers don't jive." There's no connection between the two words. The jargon of jazz musicians in the 1920s and 1930s was known as **jive.** The word **jive** was then attached to a certain a type of jazz/swing music and dance. **Jive** also came to be associated with deceptive or foolish talk. (*Don't jive me, man.*) To talk **jive** can mean just to fool around, exaggerate, joke or tease with language. However, it can also be used in an extremely derogatory manner as in **jive-*ss m*th*r-f*ck*r**—a term that was abbreviated to *JAMF.* According to Robert S. Gold in *Jazz Talk,* the abbreviation originated with saxophonist Charlie Parker.

❏

genus / genius

A **genus** is a general kind or group of something or, in biology, a taxonomic group containing one or more species.

> ❏ The female of the **genus** homo is economically dependent on the male. He is her food supply—Charlotte Perkins Gilman

A **genius** is a person of exceptional talents or aptitude, more specifically someone of vastly superior intellect and creativity.

> ❏ **Genius** is more often found in a cracked pot than in a whole one. —E.B. White

❏

grate / great

Grate means:

○ A framework of metal bars.

   ❑ The leading cause of death among fashion models is falling through street **grates**.—Dave Barry

   ❑ I wonder why they don't put some lumps of ice in the **grate**? You fill it with lumps of coal in the winter, you know, and you sit round it and enjoy the warmth. How jolly it would be to fill it now with lumps of ice, and sit round it and enjoy the coolth!
—Lewis Carroll

○ Scrape or shred.

   ❑ I want a dish to taste good, rather than to have been seethed in pig's milk and served wrapped in a rhubarb leaf with **grated** thistle root.
—Kingsley Amis

○ A harsh rasping sound (noun) or to make such a sound (verb).

   ❑ I had rather be a kitten and cry mew
I had rather hear a brazen canstick turned,
Or a dry wheel **grate** on the axle-tree,
And that would set my teeth nothing on edge,
Nothing so much as mincing poetry.
'Tis like the forced gait of a shuffling nag.—William Shakespeare

Great means "extraordinary or outstanding."

   ❑ **Great** things are won by **great** dangers.—Herodotus

---

TANGENT: Shakespeare Had a Way With Words

In the above, the Bard used "brazen canstick" to poetically refer to a "brass candlestick," but we commonly use many less poetic terms coined by William Shakespeare (1564–1616). Bardophiles estimate Willy the Shake added about 1,500 (perhaps more) words to the English language. Some, like *silly* (he meant "innocent"), have shifted meaning. Others, like *bisson* ("blind"), are no longer used. There are still hundreds, like *advertising, blanket, elbow, label,* and *unreal,* in daily use. We also use scores of Shakespearian phrases every day. It is from the phrase here (*Henry IV*)—"set my teeth nothing on edge"—that we get our "set my/your teeth on edge." "Bated breath" (*Merchant of Venice*), "wild-goose chase" (*Romeo and Juliet*), and "in a pickle" (*Tempest*) are a few more examples. In fact, if you are finding this book to be "all Greek" to you, Shakespeare coined that saying, too, in *Julius Caesar*. (See also page 125.)

❑

grisly / gristly / grizzled / grizzly

Grisly (*GRIZ-lee*) means "horrible, gruesome."

❑ The devastated landscape was a **grisly** scene of shattered concrete and torn bodies.

Gristly can sound (*GRIZ-lee*) like *grisly*, but is usually pronounced *GRIS-lee* because it is based on the word *gristle* and means containing or characterized by gristle, the cartilage found in meat.

❑ The steak was tough and **gristly**.

Grizzled (*GRIZ-uhld*) describes hair that is gray, graying, flecked or partly gray, so it also means, by extension, old. And **grizzly** (GRIZ-lee) is another word for **grizzled**, but *grizzled* is more frequently used.

❑ His hair just **grizzled**, as in a green old age.—John Dryden

The **grizzly** bear (or just *grizzly* without the *bear*) has thick fur that varies from light brown to nearly black. Long hairs on the bear's shoulder and back are often frosted with white. This coloration has given them the name *silvertip* as well as *grizzly*—the bear is named for his appearance rather than his horrible demeanor. Ironically, the scientific name for the *grizzly* is *Ursus horribilis*, which DOES mean "horrible bear" in Latin.

❑ The **grizzly** population is only about 1,000 in the lower 48 states—reduced from an estimated 50,000 to 100,000 before the West was settled.

❑

gorilla / guerrilla

A **gorilla** is a large primate.

❑ Fewer than 650 mountain **gorillas** and 40,000 lowland **gorillas** are left in the world.

A **guerrilla** is a member of an irregular armed force that fights a stronger force by sabotage and harassment.

❑ The conventional army loses if it does not win. The **guerrilla** wins if he does not lose.—Henry Kissinger

Acquired from Spanish during the [Iberian] Peninsular War (1808–1814)—*guerrilla*="skirmish, raid" (literally "little war"), a diminutive of *guerra* ("war")—the word should properly be *guerrillero* ("fighter"). That little battle, as H.W. Fowler admitted in *MEU* (1926), has long been lost. There was also much debate over the spelling—one *r* or two. Fowler also felt the double-*r* partisans had lost, but now *guerrilla* is used far more than *guerilla*. Is there hope for *guerrillero*?

❑

ground zero

Shortly after the first atomic test in Alamogordo, New Mexico on 16 July 1945, Manhattan Project physicist Philip Morrison, an eyewitness, wrote an account beginning: "I observed the Trinity shot looking toward Zero from a position on the south bank of the base camp reservoir directly beside the larger water tank." One other eyewitness referred to *zero point*. The *zero* to which they referred was the location of a 100-foot steel tower that was marked as *zero* on maps used by test engineers. The bomb detonated that day sat on a platform atop the tower. The blast wave of the explosion was calculated in relation to the lateral distance from the map coordinates. No mention of the phrase **ground zero** was made in the War Department's press release concerning the event or in the official memorandum made to the Secretary of War. A U.S. Army photo of the remains of a tower footing is labeled only as "ZERO." Radiation and other test monitoring documents from the project use *zero* to indicate the detonation point.

In a document from the U.S. Strategic Bombing Survey titled *The Effects of the Atomic Bombings of Hiroshima and Nagasaki* dated 19 June 1946, the following is found:

> ...some reinforced concrete buildings collapsed and suffered structural damage when within 2,000 feet of ground zero, and some internal wall paneling was demolished even up to 3,800 feet. (For convenience, the term "ground zero" will be used to designate the point on the ground directly beneath the point of detonation, or "air zero".)

Hanson W. Baldwin used the phrase *ground zero* in a *New York Times* report on 7 July 1946. "The intense heat of the blast started fires as far as 3,500 feet from 'ground zero' the point on the ground directly under the bomb's explosion in the air." The *Oxford English Dictionary* still refers to *ground zero* as "that part of the ground situated immediately under an exploding bomb, esp. an atomic one." The phrase, however, quickly came to mean the point of impact of any missile or bomb, especially a nuclear bomb.

By extension, *ground zero* came to mean the center of intense change or rapid development, as in: *The more rippable North Shore venues became* **ground zero** *for progressive surfing*. More appropriately, it was used to connote the center of any catastrophe or great effort, as in: **Ground zero** *in the Colombian drug war* and *AIDS Researchers Meet at* **Ground Zero**: *South Africa*. Figuratively, it was also used synonymously with *square one* as in *we're back to* **square one** and *starting at* **square one**. (Considering the original meaning, we never felt this was either a good place from which to start or go back to.)

It is unclear who first used the phrase in relation to the terrorist attacks of 11 September 2001. Some have theorized first use came in connection with the Pentagon attack since the term had a previously established connection to the building.

⇨

ground zero (continued)

Since 1943, the U.S. Department of Defense has been housed in a pentagon-shaped building in Washington, DC—the shape became the name: the Pentagon. During the Cold War Pentagon employees, realizing the building was the obvious target of the Soviet Union's first volley in a nuclear war, dubbed a hamburger stand in the center courtyard *Ground Zero*. This blackly humorous appellation was eventually extended to mean the entire building.

This paragraph appeared in a story by Dave Moniz and Andrea Stone headlined *As Pentagon watched NYC news, 'boom!'* in *USAToday* from 12 September 2001:
> "I knew this was always called **Ground Zero**, but I thought it was inviolate," said Marsha Reid, 29, a defense contractor. "I had no idea I would be in the middle of a war zone."

However, these four stories from the *New York Times* of the same day, 12 September 2001, used the phrase in three different contexts. Three of the four used it in direct reference to the site of the World Trade Center:

1. From: *A Day of Terror: Washington; Stunned Tourists, Gridlocked Streets, Fleeing and Fear* by Francis X. Clines:
> "I wanted to come out to look at **ground zero** of this country," said the man, Wes Myers, a scientist from the University of California who is working for the Department of Energy. "I had to see the Washington Monument and the U.S. Capitol that symbolize the core of this nation." ... Mr. Myers sounded grief-stricken as he looked about. "They're still here," he said, nodding appreciatively.

2. From: *A Day of Terror: Hospitals; Pictures of Medical Readiness, Waiting and Hoping for Survivors to Fill Their Wards*, by Dan Barry:
> But **ground zero**, as it was being called by hospital workers and police officers, was Lower Manhattan—

3. From: *A Day of Terror: The Reaction; A Tough City is Swept by Anger, Despair and Helplessness*, by Jim Dwyer and Susan Sachs:
> As those brushed by the attacks drifted away from the neighborhood around **ground zero**, they were met with acts of grace, large and small.

4. From: *A Day of Terror: The Media; As an Attack Unfolds, a Struggle to Provide Vivid Images to Homes*, by Felicity Barringer And Geraldine Fabrikant:
> Because New York was not just **ground zero** of the opening attack but also the heartland of the media industry, some of the most dramatic early accounts were from correspondents working at or near their homes.

⇨

ground zero (continued)

The *Washington Post* did not use the phrase *ground zero* until the following day, 13 September 2001. The instance referred to the capital city being long-considered as *ground zero*. The other two refer to the WTC site as *ground zero*:

1. From: *A Day of Courage, Patriotism, Anxiety; Workers put on a brave face In An Attempt At Normality*, by Lyndsey Layton:
    For years, many people supposed Washington would be "**ground zero**" in a terrorist attack, and now it had happened.

2. From: *Falling: Buildings, Ash, Hope and Tears Lurking in the Debris, Danger Postpones Moment of Truth*, by Michael Powell and Sally Jenkins:
    [NEW YORK] Now the stuff is airborne and the Environmental Protection Agency today took measurements at **ground zero** and found four times the acceptable level.

3. From: *Leaders in the Breach* [Column] by Mary McGrory:
    The outstanding political figure in the landscape of death and pain was, hands down, Rudy Giuliani, the mayor of New York. For those who find His Honor abrasive and even fascist, it was a surprise to find themselves waiting for his return to the screen. He was at **ground zero,** as is his wont. He stood in the rubble, his suit covered with white ash from the horrendous explosions. He dispensed reassurance to his people, defied the maniacs who had maimed his city and talked sense to the country.

The phrase *ground zero* is now definitely established in the public vocabulary as referring to the scene of mass devastation in New York City where the World Trade Center once stood. The similar attack on the Pentagon—resulting in damage that was repaired within a year—has never been referred to as *ground zero*.

According to a 24 February 2002 article by Janny Scott in the *New York Times*, Steve Kleinedler, a senior editor for the *American Heritage College Dictionary* (Fourth Edition) said no new meaning had been added to their entry on *ground zero*. The editors choose to wait and see whether the phrase "will turn out to merit its own sense." Jesse Sheidlower, the principal editor of the North American editorial unit of the *Oxford English Dictionary*, said "*Ground zero* is probably too specific, though it's a possibility. We have it in the nuclear sense."

An informal survey of publications in early 2003 found that no standard had yet been established for capitalization of the term. The Associated Press, *New York Times, Time* magazine, *Denver Post*, and *Boston Globe* are among those using *ground zero*—all lowercase. *Wall Street Journal, The New Yorker* magazine, *Hartford Courant, Houston Chronicle, London Times, Publishers Weekly* and others capitalize the two words: *Ground Zero*.

❑

❧H❧

hail / hale

Hail means:

○ Salute, greet or call.

❏ And forever, brother, **hail** and farewell. *(Atque in perpetuum, frater, ave atque vale.)*—Catullus

○ Small pellets of ice which fall from the sky like rain and, by extension, a *hail* of things means a lot of them are being directed toward someone all at once.

❏ Thou art a beaten dog beneath the **hail**...—Ezra Pound

❏ He appears to me to have lived in a **hail** of saucepan-lids. His whole existence was a scuffle.—Charles Dickens

Hale means "healthy and strong."

❏ "You are old, Father William," the young man cried,
"The few locks which are left you are gray;
You are **hale**, Father William, a hearty old man,—
Now tell me the reason I pray."—Robert Southey

The phrase **hail from** means to come or originate from. (As in *She hails from Alabama*.)

Tangent: Hail-Fellows!

Hail fellow well met, all dirty and wet;
Find out, if you can, who's master, who's man.—Jonathan Swift

The idiom *Hail fellow, well met!* is more than just an archaic greeting. *Hail-fellow* and *hail-fellow-well-met* (with or without hyphens) are used as nouns for "a heartily sociable (perhaps overly so) man" and as adverbs meaning "enthusiastically congenial." It also has a meaning of "on familiar, friendly terms" as in this 18th century example: "You see the highest quality and the lowest trades-folk jostling each other, without ceremony, *hail-fellow well met*." ⇨

Tangent (continued)

According to the *OED*, the phrase can also mean "over familiar or unduly intimate" and gives this 1688 citation: "Let not your Servants be over-familiar or *haile fellow* with you." There also seems to be a general meaning of "a good guy" or "regular fellow." ("Your 2003 U.S. Open champion is a *hail-fellow-well-met,* so let's give Jim Furyk his due. Heck, Furyk is such a regular guy that he doesn't even care that his caddy...is more famous."—Seth Davis, *Sports Ilustrated.* "How many hands he shook, how many people he was *'hale-fellow-well-met'* with, it is impossible to guess!"—Jules Verne (English translation by Mercier and King, 1873) in *From the Earth to the Moon.* "...a good manner was a primary asset, here a man must be even more free and easy, *hail-fellow-well-met,* drink, gamble, go to the horse-races, mix well, or he had no chance... As a barrister he was a failure and resentful at his failure not understanding why some cheerful, *hail-fellow-well-met* young rival with half his brain was always full of briefs and work and he went idle."—From *Grey Steel,* a biography of Jan Christian Smuts by H.C. Armstrong (1939)]

❑

hall / haul

A **hall** is a passageway or a large room or building for meetings or entertainment.

❑ vanished into nowhere Zen New Jersey leaving a trail of ambiguous picture postcards of Atlantic City **Hall**—Allen Ginsberg

Haul means:

○ To pull, drag or transport.

❑ If any one attempts to **haul** down the American flag, shoot him on the spot.—John A. Dix

○ The amount of something obtained.

❑ Archeologist Heinrich Schliemann, who knew the works of Homer by heart, proclaimed, "I have seen the face of Agamemnon" after uncovering a gold mask among the huge **haul** of ancient artifacts.

○ A period of time.

❑ Over the long **haul** of life on this planet, it is the ecologists, and not the bookkeepers of business, who are the ultimate accountants. —Stewart L. Udall

❑

hanged / hung

Hanged is used as the past tense and a past participle of *hang* when referring to death by hanging.

❏ "Many men have been **hanged** on far slighter evidence," I remarked. "So they have. And many men have been wrongfully **hanged**." —Arthur Conan Doyle

Hung is the preferred past tense and a past participle of *hang* for any other meaning (such as "suspended or supported from above; attached to wall").

❏ The ships **hung** in the sky in much the same way that bricks don't. —Douglas Adams

❐

hear / here

Hear means "to perceive by ear."

❏ Whenever I **hear** the word culture, I reach for my revolver. —Hermann Goering

Here means "in this place."

❏ A billion **here**, a billion there, pretty soon it adds up to real money. —Everett Dirksen

❐

heard / herd

Heard is the past tense of *hear*.

❏ Writers should be read, but neither seen nor **heard**. —Daphne du Maurier

A **herd** is a group of animals

❏ A man who is free is like a mangy sheep in a **herd**. He will contaminate my entire kingdom and ruin my work.—Jean-Paul Sartre

❐

Hindi / Hindu

Hindi is a language of India. A **Hindu** is a follower of Hinduism, a religion. Not all Indians are *Hindus*, although some are. Not all *Hindus* are Indians. Not all Indians speak *Hindi*.

❑ The Buddha was born a **Hindu**. But he carried the theme of sensory indifference further, boiling it down to a severe maxim—life is suffering—and placing it in the center of his philosophy.
—Robert Wright

Be cautious when using the terms *Hindi, Urdu,* and *Hindustani.* There is disagreement about the definition of the languages. One of the more diplomatic explanations we found comes from the United Nations Department of Public Information:

Hindi is the most widely spoken language of the Republic of India... Its 275 million speakers rank it as one of the leading languages of the world but it is, nevertheless, understood by only about one third of India's population. When independence was achieved in 1947, Hindi was chosen as one of India's national languages. Like most of the languages of northern India, Hindi is a direct descendant of Sanskrit. It has been influenced and enriched by Dravidian, Turkish, Farsi, Arabic, Portuguese, and English. Hindi and Urdu, the official language of Pakistan, are virtually the same language, though the former is written in the Sanskrit characters and the latter in the Perso-Arabic script. Pure Hindi derives most of its vocabulary from Sanskrit, while Urdu contains many words from Persian and Arabic. The basis of both languages is actually Hindustani, the colloquial form of speech that served as the lingua franca of much of India for more than four centuries. Hindi was originally a variety of Hindustani spoken in the area of New Delhi. Its development into a national language had its beginnings in the colonial period, when the British began to cultivate it as a standard among government officials. Later it was used for literary purposes and has since then become the vehicle for prose and poetry.

❐

historic / historical

Something of lasting importance in the course of history is **historic**.

❑ Ireland's ruins are **historic** emotions surrendered to time.
—Horace Sutton

Anything that happens in the past, no matter how unimportant, is a **historical** event. *Historical* also refers to anything related to the study of the past.

❑ A **historical** romance is the only kind of book where chastity really counts.—Barbara Cartland

❐

hoard / horde

A **hoard** is a store of something valuable. It can also be used as a verb.

- ❑ Smaug's lair was filled with a great **hoard** of stolen treasure.

- ❑ The sage does not **hoard**. Having bestowed all he has on others, he has yet more; Having given all he has to others, he is richer still.—Lao-Tzu

A **horde** is a large group or crowd.

- ❑ With James, Earl of Bothwell by her side, Mary Queen of Scots led a motley **horde** of followers against the rebellious nobles at Carberry Hill, but no battle ensued.

hole / whole

A **hole** is an opening or empty space.

- ❑ Love is a **hole** in the heart.—Ben Hecht

Whole means "to be complete or entire."

- ❑ This **whole** world is wild at heart and weird on top.—David Lynch

hopefully

Using hopefully to mean "in a hopeful manner" is unquestionably correct.

- ❑ To travel **hopefully** is a better thing than to arrive. —Robert Louis Stevenson

The problem arises when the word is used in a sentence like *Hopefully, this entry will be short* meaning "it is to be hoped that the entry will be short." The dispute began in the U.S. in the late 60s and has now calmed down somewhat, but discussion of the matter still inevitably results in endless contention. We refuse to enter the fray. Instead we quote word maven William Safire: "The word 'hopefully' has become the litmus test to determine whether one is a language snob or a language slob." We wish to be neither.

I

ideal / idle / idol / idyll

An **ideal** is an image of perfection or excellence.

- There is no dream of love, however **ideal** it may be, which does not end up with a fat, greedy baby hanging from the breast. —Charles Baudelaire

Idle means "inactive or ineffective; not employed or busy; lazy; lacking substance, value, or basis."

- **Idle** youth, enslaved to everything; by being too sensitive I have wasted my life.—Arthur Rimbaud

An **idol** is a person who is greatly admired or respected, or an object or image which is worshipped as a god.

- They wouldn't be heroes if they were infallible, in fact they wouldn't be heroes if they weren't miserable wretched dogs, the pariahs of the earth, besides which the only reason to build up an **idol** is to tear it down again.—Lester Bangs

An **idyll** is a happy, peaceful, and simple situation or period of time, or a piece of music, literature, or art that describes this

- A play will be performed in Germany, compared to which the French Revolution will seem a mere inoffensive **idyll.**—Heinrich Heine

imply / infer

The Short and Sweet Version

Speakers and writers **imply** something by hinting at it or suggesting rather than stating directly. Listeners and readers **infer** something from what they hear or read; they come to a conclusion based on facts.

- From a drop of water a logician could **infer** the possibility of an Atlantic or a Niagara without having seen or heard of one or the other. —Arthur Conan Doyle

⇨

❑ Words like "freedom," "justice," "democracy" are not common concepts; on the contrary, they are rare. People are not born knowing what these are. It takes enormous and, above all, individual effort to arrive at the respect for other people that these words **imply**.
—James Baldwin

A Further Note on *Imply/Infer*

Imply can also have a negative overtone. Even though the speaker/writer is not actually asserting it, there's a suggestion that whatever is being *implied* is somewhat improper. *I wasn't sure what she was implying, but it didn't sound good.* When you *imply* things about someone, you are generally saying something not to that person's credit.

❑ Writing prejudicial, off-putting reviews is a precise exercise in applied black magic. The reviewer can draw free-floating disagreeable associations to a book by **implying** that the book is completely unimportant without saying exactly why, and carefully avoiding any clear images that could capture the reader's full attention.—William Burroughs

The "Confound the Experts" Version Involving *Imply/Infer*

Usage mavens will sternly state, "*Infer* is often misused for *imply*. The words are not interchangeable." This has not, however, always been the case. Don't take *our* word for it. Here's an expert explanation:

Sir Thomas More is the first writer known to have used both *infer* and *imply* in their approved senses (1528). He is also the first to have used *infer* in a sense close in meaning to *imply* (1533). Both of these uses of *infer* coexisted without comment until some time around the end of World War I. Since then, senses 3 ["**a**: to involve as a normal outcome of thought **b**: to point out: **INDICATE** <this doth *infer* the zeal I had to see him—Shakespeare>..."] and 4 ["**SUGGEST, HINT** <are you *inferring* I'm incompetent? >"] of *infer* have been frequently condemned as an undesirable blurring of a useful distinction. The actual blurring has been done by the commentators. Sense 3, descended from More's use of 1533, does not occur with a personal subject. When objections arose, they were to a use with a personal subject (now sense 4). Since dictionaries did not recognize this use specifically, the objectors assumed that sense 3 was the one they found illogical, even though it had been in respectable use for four centuries.
The actual usage condemned was a spoken one never used in logical discourse. At present sense 4 is found in print chiefly in letters to the editor and other informal prose, not in serious intellectual writing. The controversy over sense 4 has apparently reduced the frequency of use of sense 3. ["infer." *Merriam-Webster Online Dictionary*. 2003.]

◗

impracticable / impractical

Impracticable is an adjective that refers to a course of action that is impossible to carry out or put into practice. (It can also mean "impassable.")

❑ Resolve not to be poor: whatever you have, spend less. Poverty is a great enemy to human happiness; it certainly destroys liberty, and it makes some virtues **impracticable**, and others extremely difficult.
—Samuel Johnson

Impractical can be synonymous with impracticable, but it really has a somewhat weaker meaning. It suggests that it might not make sense to carry out an action or continue it or that there is a lack of ability to act prudently or sensibly.

❑ More than an end to war, we want an end to the beginning of all wars —yes, an end to this brutal, inhuman and thoroughly **impractical** method of settling the differences between governments.
—Franklin D. Roosevelt

❑

in / in to / into

In indicates location.

❑ Without censorship, things can get terribly confused **in** the public mind.—General William Westmoreland

In to is two words, an adverb and a preposition; *in* modifies a verb, adjective or other adverb:

❑ I will never give **in to** old age until I become old. And I'm not old yet!
—Tina Turner

Into indicates motion.

❑ So she ran **into** the bedroom
She was struck down,
it was her doom—Michael Jackson

❑

indict / indite

Indict means "to formally accuse."

❑ If the district attorney wanted, a grand jury would **indict** a ham sandwich.—Barry Slotnick

Indite means "write down or compose."

❑ Language has not the power to speak what love **indites**: The Soul lies buried in the ink that writes.—John Clare

❑

indigenous / indigent / indignant

Indigenous means "native."

- ❑ The term Hispanic, coined by technomarketing experts and by the designers of political campaigns, homogenizes our cultural diversity (Chicanos, Cubans, and Puerto Ricans become indistinguishable), avoids our **indigenous** cultural heritage and links us directly with Spain. Worse yet, it possesses connotations of upward mobility and political obedience.—Guillermo Gomez-Pena

Indigent means "impoverished, destitute."

- ❑ Democracy is when the **indigent**, and not the men of property, are the rulers.—Aristotle

Indignant means "righteously angry."

- ❑ I understand the inventor of the bagpipes was inspired when he saw a man carrying an **indignant**, asthmatic pig under his arm. Unfortunately, the manmade sound never equaled the purity of the sound achieved by the pig.—Alfred Hitchcock

❑

ingenious / ingenuous

Ingenious means "clever, imaginative, inventive."

- ❑ An inventor is a person who makes an **ingenious** arrangement of wheels, levers and springs, and believes it civilization.—Ambrose Bierce

Ingenuous means "candid, frank, guileless."

- ❑ I don't judge a regime by the damning criticism of the opposition, but by the **ingenuous** praise of the partisan.—Jean Rostand

❑

ironic / irony / ironically

We can't blame Alanis Morissette's lyrics to "Ironic" for the rampant misuse of **ironic**. People commonly misapply **ironic**, **irony**, and **ironically** to events and situations that should be described as *coincidental* or *improbable*. H.W. Fowler, with his usual directness, wrote in *The King's English* (1908): "The word irony is one of the worst abused in the language... Now any definition of irony—though hundreds might be given, and very few of them would be accepted—must include this, that the surface meaning and the underlying meaning of what is said are not the same." More specifically, we might define irony as "the use of language to mean something quite opposite from what the words literally say." We might also tell you more in the following *Tangent.*

⇨

TANGENT: It's, Like, Cosmic

We have a theory. We think this misunderstanding of **irony** arises as a result of learning a little something about *literary irony* (probably as a freshman in high school) and then getting confused. In literary terms, irony means "deliberate incongruity between the language used and what is being discussed." Although you will find various breakdowns, types, and definitions of irony (including *dramatic, Socratic,* and *romantic irony*), we found it easiest to consider four major types of irony:

1. **Verbal irony** refers to spoken words only. A character says one thing, but suggests or intends the opposite. In *Julius Caesar,* Mark Antony says "and Brutus is an honorable man" repeatedly in his funeral oration for Caesar. He is implying that Brutus is just the opposite—dishonorable because he conspired against and murdered his friend, Caesar.

Some will suggest that irony in general and verbal irony in particular are simply fancier ways of saying *sarcasm*. Sarcasm, however, is more direct, harsh, caustic, and cutting. Verbal irony is implied. George Bernard Shaw was being sarcastic with his remark: "She had lost the art of conversation, but not, unfortunately, the power of speech."

2. **Dramatic irony** depends on the structure of a work as well as words. The contrast is between what an unwitting character says, thinks, or does and the true situation. In our example above, Antony calls Brutus "honorable" *knowing* he is exactly the opposite. Another Shakespearian character, Othello, refers to his trusted friend Iago as "honest Iago." Othello believes what he says. He has no idea that Iago is a deceitful villain. Othello kills his wife, Desdemona, because he believes Iago's lies about her unfaithfulness. Othello cannot see or understand the contrast, but the audience or reader can.

One way to create dramatic irony is to allow the audience to know what is happening before the characters do. When we are watching a horror film, we know characters are doomed (or at least in for a scare) if they open that door, accept that ride from a stranger, decide to spend the night in the cemetery, or do any of a number of other dumb things the characters never seem to know not to do.

3. With **situational irony** the contrast is between what is expected (or appropriate) and what actually happens. In Shakespeare's *Macbeth,* the witches summon apparitions who tell Macbeth "none of woman born shall harm" him and that he "shall never vanquish'd be until Great Birnam Wood to high Dunsinane Hill shall come against him." Macbeth interprets this to mean he will never be harmed and never defeated. The audience knows he is wrong, but they aren't sure how this will be played out. (The ultimate irony in the play is that Macbeth hears what he wishes to hear. By believing his interpretation of the prophecies his murderous

⇨

Tangent (continued)

ambitions are made even stronger. He thinks he is invulnerable which, of course, makes him truly vulnerable.)

4. **Cosmic irony** (or **irony of fate**) is pessimistic and fatalistic. (It can be seen as "really big" situational irony.) It suggests that we are mere playthings of universal forces. Fate, destiny, God, greatly evolved aliens on a higher plane of existence, the stars, or the like shape events and inspire false hope or expectations that are then destroyed. *Oedipus Rex* by Sophocles is full of all sorts of irony, but cosmic irony is its basic theme. The Chorus ends the play by pointing out the obvious:

Look ye, countrymen and Thebans, this is Oedipus the great,
He who knew the Sphinx's riddle and was mightiest in our state.
Who of all our townsmen gazed not on his fame with envious eyes?
Now, in what a sea of troubles sunk and overwhelmed he lies!
Therefore wait to see life's ending ere thou count one mortal blest;
Wait till free from pain and sorrow he has gained his final rest.
—from the W.B. Yeats translation (1928)

Or, in the vernacular, "No matter how rich and powerful you are, you can be brought down. Nobody can be called 'happy' until he is dead."

With cosmic irony, we are fairly close to what people commonly (and mistakenly) mean when they use the word *irony.*

⊓

Islam / Islamic / Muslim (see also "Moslem" / Muslim)

From *Teaching about Islam & Muslims in the Public School Classroom: A Handbook for Educators* produced by the Council on Islamic Education:

Islam is the name of the religion... *Muslim* is the name used for an adherent of the Islamic faith... The term Islamic is accurately applied only to what pertains directly to the faith and its doctrines (such as Islamic law, Islamic worship, Islamic celebrations, Islamic values, principles and beliefs.)... we may not describe a person or any historical phenomenon as Islamic.... The simplest solution is to use the terms "Islam" and "Islamic" solely for what pertains to the religion, and use Muslim as an adjective to denote the works and acts of Muslims, or groups of people and their institutions (such as Muslim women or men, Muslim populations, Muslim countries or civilization, Muslim art, Muslim government or leaders or Muslim extremists). The important distinction is that human interpretation of Islam by Muslims is necessarily imperfect and that persons, cultural artifacts and institutions are derived from and informed by Islamic precepts with a mixture of secular, regional and ethnic influences. In short, human acts and constructs fall short of being purely Islamic therefore may not be denoted as such.

⊓

it's / its

It's is a contraction of *it is*.

❑   It's not what you pay a man, but what he costs you that counts.
  —Will Rogers

Its means "belonging to it."

❑   Peace is its own reward.— Mohandas Gandhi

Simple, isn't it? Yet using **it's** instead of **its** is one of the most common mistakes made in English. There's even a newsgroup dedicated to the problem: alt.possessive.its.has.no.apostrophe.

Tips:

❍ Apostrophes are used to show possession, except with possessive pronouns like *his, hers, ours, theirs,* and *its.*

❍ Apostrophes stand in for missing letters in contractions—*it's* means "it is" or "it has" and that's it. Try substituting *it is* in place of *its* in a sentence. Does the sentence make sense? Then use *it's.*

❍ Know all this perfectly well (as we do), but *still* make typos (as we do)? Try using your word processor's FIND function and locate all the *it's* and *its* to double check.

❑

judgment / judgement

Judgment is the standard U.S. spelling; **judgement** is the British spelling. Even the English are beginning to abandon the *e,* though. Consistency is all well and good, but this is an instance where the Brits simply make more sense. (The British system of single and double quotation marks is another.) There are over three dozen other words (like *acknowledgement, arrangement, engagement*) in which the a soft *g* sound before *-ment* occurs with an *e.* Words like *segment* and *pigment* omit the *e* and have the hard *g* sound. Why not *judgement?* Probably due to that stodgy old Noah Webster. (He wasn't right on everything. He wanted to change *women* to *wimmen.*)

But—unless you are also using *colour, kerb, tyre, cheque,* etc.— you'd best drop the *e.*

❑ Slowly he entered dark and silence and lay there for so long that with what **judgement** remained he judged them to be final.—Samuel Beckett

❐

Jew / Jewish / Hebrew

The appropriate word for a modern **Jewish** person is **Jew** and for the people, **Jews.** *Jew* is the correct noun for either males or females. (*Jewess* is to be avoided.) Use *Jewish* as the adjective. *Hebrew* is the name of an ancient Canaanitic language that is now the official language of Israel, the Jewish state. Using *Hebrew* to describe a person is not acceptable.

❑ Yes, I am a **Jew,** and when the ancestors of the right honourable gentleman were brutal savages in an unknown island, mine were priests in the temple of Solomon.—Benjamin Disraeli

❐

kudos

Kudos means "praise" or "credit for an achievement." It comes from a Greek word, *kydos*, for "glory" and is singular: *Kudos is deserved for your effort.* We feel there's no such word as *kudo*—even though *Merriam-Webster* claims it exists.

The *Merriam-Webster Online Dictionary (2003)* asserts *kudo* "is simply one of the most recent words created by back-formation from another word misunderstood as a plural." It defends this use of *kudos* and even the singular form *kudo,* on the grounds that these adaptations follow the same pattern of words such as *pea.*

Peas started out as a singular word with no plural. If it had remained so, there would have been *peas-shooters*, the flower would be *a sweet peas,* and there would be peas-sized objects and amounts. English-speakers, noting the *s* on the end, mistook *peas* for a plural and began referring to one *pea* and many *peas*. This process is called **back-formation:** the creation of a new word from an existing word based on the pattern of existing pairs of words that show the same pattern of construction. That's how, back in the 15th century, we got *cobbler* from *cobble* and later coined *televise* from *television* (1950), as well as about a thousand other perfectly acceptable words.

Kudos was introduced as British university slang in the 18th or 19th century. The college lads pronounced it *KYOO-dahs* and— since reading and writing both Latin and Greek were required of the educated mind in those days—they knew it was singular.

Fluency in classical Greek declined, however, and eventually folks (particularly Yanks) started pronouncing it *KOO-doz*. This made it *sound* plural. By the 1920s *kudos* began to appear as a plural. By 1945 *kudo* began to appear.

Despite Henry Luce and his *Time*-style vocabulary, misguided sportswriters, and others, the standard remains: *kudos* is singular; *kudo* is imaginary. As R.W. Burchfield writes in *The New Fowler's Modern English Usage* (1998): "It is true that back-formations resulting from a misinterpretation of the function of a final -*s* can be found... But this is an old discarded process. No other word of Greek origin (*bathos, chaos, pathos,* etc.) has suffered such an undignified fate."

❧ L ❧

laps / lapse

Laps is the plural of *lap*.

- ❑ They'll take suggestion as a cat **laps** milk.—William Shakespeare
- ❑ I've been in more **laps** than a napkin.—Mae West

Lapse can mean "to fall from a higher standard."

- ❑ It is the creative nature of man which has refused to let him **lapse** back into that unconscious unity with life which characterizes the animal world from which he made his escape.—Henry Miller

Lapse can also mean "temporary failure."

- ❑ Somebody once said that I am incapable of drawing a man, but that I draw abstract things like despair, disillusion, despondency, sorrow, **lapse** of memory, exile, and that these things are sometimes in a shape that might be called Man or Woman.—James Thurber

"Passage of time" is another meaning for **lapse**.

- ❑ Concessions are essential at the outset of marital life, but after a certain **lapse** of time you can't afford to lose any more ground.—Jean Rostand

❐

lath / lathe

Lath is a narrow thin strip of wood used to back plaster or make latticework.

- ❑ England seemed a great house with every room portioned by **lath** and plaster.—Gaston Bachelard

A **lathe** is a machine tool for shaping metal or wood; the work piece turns about a horizontal axis against a fixed tool.

- ❑ Those whom heaven helps we call the sons of heaven. They do not learn this by learning. They do not work it by working. They do not reason it by using reason. To let understanding stop at what cannot be understood is a high attainment. Those who cannot do it will be destroyed on the **lathe** of heaven.—Chuang Tse

❐

lay / lie

Lay means "to put or place something or someone down." *Lay* is a transitive verb. (Your school teacher called it an "action verb.") A transitive verb requires a direct object to complete its meaning. (Someone or something receives the action of the verb. The person or thing that receives its action is the direct object.)

- ❏ Please *lay* **it** on the examination table.
- ❏ Mark *laid* the mutilated **body** in the rough grave.

Lie means "to rest or recline." *Lie* is an intransitive verb. It cannot take a direct object. (It's still an action verb, but the action ends instead of being transferred to some person or object or the action is modified by an adverb or adverb phrase.)

- ❏ She *lies* in her coffin now.
- ❏ Please, just let past indiscretions *lie*.

Part of the confusion comes because the present tense of **to lay** is **lay** and the past tense of **to lie** is ALSO **lay**. And when I *lie* down (present tense, intransitive), I can be said to *lay* my body down (present tense, transitive).

Still confused? Okay, imagine what is happening. If you are referring to something being **placed**, then the correct word would be a form of **lay**. If you are referring to something **reclining** or **resting**, then the correct would be a form of **lie**.

- ❏ I will take the lilies and *lay* them on her grave. (The lilies are getting *placed*.)
- ❏ The lilies lie on her grave. (The lilies are *resting* there.)

There is another **lie**, of course, as in "to falsify":

- ❏ Today I *lie* to my wife.
- ❏ Yesterday I *lied* to my wife.
- ❏ I have *lied* to my wife.

Although this type of lying can get you into more trouble than incorrect grammar ever could, at least the verb form is simple to deal with.

❐

lead / led

Lead can be pronounced two ways.

The *noun* that rhymes with *dead* means (among other things) "a soft heavy toxic malleable metallic element."

❑ God keep **lead** out of me!—William Shakespeare

Although there is it is a mixture of graphite and clay, the marking substance in a pencil is called a *lead.*

The *noun* that rhymes with *deed* means (among other things):

○ The playing of a card to start a trick in bridge.

❑ **Lead** the jack and let it ride.

○ Leadership.

❑ There is nothing more difficult to take in hand, more perilous to conduct or more uncertain in its success than to take the **lead** in the introduction of a new order of things.—Niccolo Machiavelli

○ Principal role or the person who plays it.

❑ She played the **lead** on the BBC series.

○ A position at the front.

❑ Our horse took the **lead** in the stretch and pulled away to win the race.

○ Evidence pointing to a possible solution.

❑ Police followed several **leads** to find the perpetrators.

○ A news story of major importance.

❑ The arrest made national headlines and was the **lead** in many papers.

○ A leash.

❑ The dog **lead** is constructed from top-grain leather.

○ An indication of potential opportunity.

❑ Mavis gave me a **lead** on a good job.

○ Position taken by a base runner off a base toward the next.

❑ Morgan took a "one foot on the carpet" **lead** off first base.

The *verb* **lead** that rhymes with *deed* means (among other things):

○ To show the way.

❑ The paths of glory **lead** but to the grave.—Thomas Gray

⇨

○ To control a group; to be the person who makes the decisions or the most important in a group.

❑ Once **lead** this people into war and they will forget there ever was such a thing as tolerance.—Woodrow Wilson

○ To be in front, to be first or to be winning.

❑ On matters of race, on matters of decency, baseball should **lead** the way.—A. Bartlett Giamatti

○ To cause (someone) to do something.

❑ **Lead** the audience by the nose to the thought.—Laurence Olivier

○ To pass or spend.

❑ The mass of men **lead** lives of quiet desperation.
—Henry David Thoreau

The past tense and past participle of the *verb* is **led**, which rhymes with *dead*.

❑ The nose of a mob is its imagination. By this, at any time, it can be quietly **led**.—Edgar Allan Poe

❐

lean / lien

Lean can mean:

○ Tilt, incline.

❑ Laws, like houses, **lean** on one another.—Edmund Burke

○ Thin.

❑ Let me have men about me that are fat,
Sleek-headed men, and such as sleep a-nights.
Yon Cassius has a **lean** and hungry look;
He thinks too much. Such men are dangerous.—William Shakespeare

A **lien** is a legal claim on someone's property.

❑ If there is a **lien** against your car, it may be seized to pay off the previous owner's debt.

❐

lightening / lightning

Lightening means:

○ Brightening up with light.

❑ That I may apprehend thee as light **lightening** every creature and everything, every moment; that I may know thee as truth, hearing thy voice; that I may serve thee as love, loving thy people, asking for no reward, no place, but one only and for one instant-to lean on thy bosom.—Eric Milner-White

○ Making lighter in weight.

❑ As on the highroad he who walks lightest walks with most ease, so on the journey of life more happiness comes from **lightening** the needs by poverty than from panting under a burden of wealth. —Marcus Minucius Felix

Lightning is the electrical charge that comes in bolts from the sky

❑ I'd rather be a **lightning** rod than a seismograph.—Ken Kesey

❑

loan / lone

Loan means "something given temporarily."

❑ Neither a borrower nor a lender be;
For **loan** oft loses both itself and friend,
And borrowing dulls the edge of husbandry.
—William Shakespeare

Lone means "solitary or unaccompanied."

❑ Did she in touching that **lone** wing
Recall the years before her mind
Became a bitter, an abstract thing...?
—William Butler Yeats

❑

loath / loathe

Loath means "averse, reluctant; unwilling" (pronounced to rhyme with *both*).

❑ I would be **loath** to speak ill of any person who I do not know deserves it, but I am afraid he is an attorney.—Samuel Johnson

Loathe means "to hate" (pronounced with a fully voiced *th* as in the word *smooth*).

❑ I nauseate walking; 'tis a country diversion; I **loathe** the country. —William Congreve

Other Forms:

Loathing (noun): hatred

❑ A general **loathing** of a gang or sect usually has some sound basis in instinct.—Ezra Pound

Loathly (adjective): highly offensive; arousing aversion or disgust

❑ Turns to meet the **loathly** birds
Flocking round him from the skies,
Waiting for the flesh that dies.—Ralph Hodgson

Loathsome (adjective)

❑ Grim death, how foul and **loathsome** is thine image.
—William Shakespeare

❐

loose / lose

Loose (as a verb) means "unfasten or set free."

❑ Cry "havoc!" and let **loose** the dogs of war,
That this foul deed shall smell above the earth
With carrion men, groaning for burial.—William Shakespeare

Loose (as an adjective) is the opposite of *tight* (and means, among other things, "lacking in morals").

❑ To be **loose** with grammar is to be **loose** with the worst woman in the world.—Otis C. Edwards

Lose means "to cease to have or become unable to find."

❑ To **lose** one parent may be regarded as a misfortune... to **lose** both seems like carelessness.—Oscar Wilde

❐

lustful / lusty

Although some dictionaries will equate the two words, **lusty** and **lustful** have distinct meanings. We admit there is some archaic overlap and modern misuse, so we caution you to always make your meaning clear through context.

Lusty means "healthy, strong, hearty, robust, vigorous" or "enthusiastic, rousing." (Archaic meanings include "attractive" and "big.")

❑ How lush and **lusty** the grass looks! How green!—William Shakespeare

❑ Though I look old, yet am I strong and **lusty**:
For in my youth I never did apply
Hot and rebellious liquors in my blood;
Nor did not with unbashful forehead woo
The means of weakness and debility:
Therefore my age is as a **lusty** winter,
Frosty, but kindly.—William Shakespeare

Lustful means "filled with sexual desire; lecherous, licentious, lewd, libidinous, lascivious..." (You get the idea.)

❑ A full stomach and warm clothing leave one free for **lustful** thoughts.
—Chinese proverb

❑ Creative times are quiet, very secretive, and **lustful**.—Ingmar Bergman

❑ The **lustful** are like frogs who, in the waters of carnal pleasure, invite one another to lust by signs and words.—Saint Anthony of Padua

❐

luxuriant / luxurious

Luxuriant means "abundant, thick, profuse, unrestrained."

❑ The soft light of a shaded lamp fell upon her as she leaned back in the basket chair, playing over her sweet grave face, and tinting with a dull, metallic sparkle the rich coils of her **luxuriant** hair.
—Arthur Conan Doyle

Luxurious means "choice and expensive, of the very best kind, full of luxury, self-indulgent."

❑ Materialism does not crowd out spiritualism; spiritualism is more likely a substitute when objects are scarce. When we have few things, we make the next world **luxurious**. When we have plenty, we enchant the objects around us.—James B. Twitchell

❐

✥M✥

main / mane

Main means "principal or chief."

❑ The **main** facts in human life are five: birth, food, sleep, love and death.—E.M. Forster

A **mane** is long hair.

❑ At fifteen I visualized myself as a world-famous author of seventy with a **mane** of wavy white hair. Today I am practically bald. —Vladimir Nabokov

manner / manor

(For related information about the homonym pair *manner/manor* see page 125)

Manner means "a way of acting or behaving."

❑ I've always felt that English women had to be approached in a sisterly **manner**, rather than an erotic **manner**.—Anthony Burgess

A **manor** is a mansion or main house on an estate.

❑ On many a **manor**-house there came evil times, and on none more than on the **Manor** of Tilford, where for many generations the noble family of the Lorings had held their home.—Arthur Conan Doyle

marital / marshal / marshall / martial

Marital means "relating to marriage."

❑ I praise wedlock, I praise **marital** union, but only because they produce me virgins.—Saint Jerome

In the U.S., **marshal** can be a title used for certain peace or fire officers. *(Wild Bill Hickok was a famous marshal of the old West.)* In some countries it is a title used for important military officers. *(Field Marshal Ferdinand Foch led the French in WW2.)* A **marshal** can also be an officer of a judicial court *(municipal court marshal)* or someone who officially organizes a public event *for (grand marshal for a*

⇨

parade). As a verb, **marshal** primarily means to gather or organize people or things.

❑ I believe women are better able to **marshal** their thoughts than men and because they are less egotistical they make fewer assumptions.
—Henry Ford

Marshal and *marshall* are both acceptable spellings, but *marshal* is the most common spelling for both the noun and verb and the accepted AP style.

Martial means "relating to the military or warlike."

❑ To a surprising extent the war-lords in shining armour, the apostles of the **martial** virtues, tend not to die fighting when the time comes. History is full of ignominious getaways by the great and famous.
—George Orwell

A military court is a **court-martial**. The plural is **courts-martial.**

The noun **material** can mean:

○ Physical substance from which things can be made.

❑ Prometheus' **material** was lowly clay, but his statues walked.
—Franz Grillparzer

○ Cloth or fabric.

❑ Never in the history of fashion has so little **material** been raised so high to reveal so much that needs to be covered so badly.—Cecil Beaton

○ Any group of ideas, sources, data, or the like that can be used to create a larger work.

❑ Doesn't all experience crumble in the end to mere literary **material**?
—Ellen Glasgow

Used as an adjective **material** means:

○ Important or directly relevant.

❑ The case was reopened on the basis of new and **material** evidence.

○ Of or pertaining to the physical or tangible rather than the spiritual or emotional

❑ I have never been a **material** girl. My father always told me never to love anything that cannot love you back.—Imelda Marcos

Materiel is equipment and supplies of an army or an organization.

❑ The Army's principal **materiel** developer is headquartered in Virginia.

❐

mat / matt / matte

We checked over a dozen dictionaries and a few specialized sources for this entry and found considerable wobbling on the matter. Most definitions would be fairly decisive, then sneak in "variant of [the other one]" at the end. Some sources claimed **matt** as an acceptable variant (especially in the U.K.) It may be semi-acceptable, but we'll stick to **mat** and **matte**.

○ The broad definition of the noun *mat* is "a covering used to protect a floor or other surface."

❑ Or on the **Mat** devoutly kneeling
Would lift her Eyes up to the Ceiling,
And heave her Bosom unaware
For neighb'ring Beaux to see it bare.—Jonathan Swift

○ As a verb, *mat* means "to entwine or alter texture into a dense tangle."

❑ And in the middle of them, with filthy body, **matted** hair, and unwiped nose, Ralph wept for the end of innocence.... William Golding

○ *Mat* can also be used to refer to a mounting consisting of a border or background for artwork.

❑ A colorful photograph looks good against a neutral **mat** of grey or tan.

○ *Matte* means not "reflecting light; lacking gloss."

❑ She preferred a soft **matte** lipstick rather than a shiny gloss lipstick.

○ In film, **matte** technique is a special effect in which part of a scene is blocked out replaced by footage containing other material (as a background painting). Digital imaging is now used for matte effects.

❑ In the late 1930s Chesley Bonestell went to work in Hollywood as a special-effects **matte** painter.

○ *Matte* is also a crude mixture that forms when sulfide metal ores are smelted

❑ Copper ore treated in a blast furnace yields a copper **matte**, from which only a part of the impurities are removed.

Mat and *matte* seem to overlap most frequently when used to describe the material or process used when mounting art. We consulted art suppliers, framers, and art publications and *mat* seems to be used more often. There was some overlap for "dull," but *matte* appears to be the choice when needing an adjective meaning "not glossy."

❐

may be / maybe

May be is a verb phrase meaning "might be" or "could be."

❑ A man **may be** so much of everything that he is nothing of anything. —Samuel Johnson

Maybe, the single word, means "perhaps."

❑ I think that **maybe** if women and children were in charge we would get somewhere.—James Thurber

❐

mean / mien

Mean, among *many* other things, means "lacking kindness."

❑ Marilyn was **mean**. Terribly mean. The meanest woman I have ever met around this town. I have never met anybody as **mean** as Marilyn Monroe or as utterly fabulous on the screen.—Billy Wilder

Mien refers to a person's manner or appearance.

❑ ...a tin-horn politician with the manner of a rural corn doctor and the **mien** of a ham actor.—H.L. Mencken

❐

meat / meet / mete

Meat is the edible flesh of an animal.

❑ Eating too much **meat** gives you indigestion and evil thoughts make you eat too much **meat**.—Gertrude Stein

Meet means, among other things, "come together or encounter."

❑ Every man I **meet** wants to protect me. I can't figure out what from. —Mae West

Mete means "to give out in measure; dole" (usually used with *out*).

❑ The worst punishment one can **mete** out is to take away someone's faith.—the *Baal Shem Tov*

❐

medal / meddle / metal / mettle

A **medal** is a small, usually *metal,* object with words and/or a picture on it, which is given as a reward for a commendable action, for excelling or achieving, or to commemorate an event or person

❑ With attractive women juries sometimes have to be restrained from handing them a **medal** for their crimes.—John McGeorge

Meddle means "intrude."

❑ Do not **meddle** in the affairs of wizards, for they are subtle and quick to anger.—J.R.R. Tolkien

Metal means "an element, such as iron or gold," or "a mixture of such elements, such as steel, which conducts electricity and heat and which is generally hard and strong."

❑ [The piano is] able to communicate the subtlest universal truths by means of wood, **metal** and vibrating air. —Kenneth Miller

Mettle means "ability and determination, courage."

❑ Bring forth men-children only;
For thy undaunted **mettle** should compose
Nothing but males.—William Shakespeare

TANGENT: Heavy Metal

Heavy metal, a scientific term concerning certain chemical properties, was evidently first used in literature by William Burroughs in *Nova Express*: "Uranian Willy the Heavy Metal Kid, also known as Willy the Rat—He wised up the marks" and "Heavy Metal People of Uranus wrapped in cool blue mist of vaporized bank notes—." Dennis Edmonton (aka Mars Bonfire) used the phrase in the lyrics of "Born to Be Wild," which was recorded by the band Steppenwolf in 1968. The phrase referred to the sound of motorcycles. Rock critic Mike Saunders claims to be the first to employ the phrase as a descriptive rock and roll term in a review of *Kingdom Come* (the first Sir Lord Baltimore album) published in the May 1971 issue of *Creem* magazine. According to Saunders, Dave Marsh coined the phrase "punk rock" in a column about a Question Mark & The Mysterians performance in the same issue.

❐

militate / mitigate

To **militate** against something is to affect or heavily influence it.

❑ The invisible powers of heaven seemed to **militate** on the side of the pious emperor.—Edward Gibbon

To **mitigate** something is to moderate it or make it less severe.

❑ The pilot cannot **mitigate** the billows or calm the winds.—Plutarch

People sometimes use *mitigate against* instead of *militate against*. This is incorrect and should be avoided. According to *Merriam-Webster,* William Faulkner used *mitigate* ("some intangible and invisible social force that mitigates against him") in this way. Although at least one critic thinks this usage should be called an American idiom, it is usually considered a mistake.

The cliché *mitigating circumstances* pops up in fictional mysteries and trial dramas as well as real university regulations. It means "circumstances that make an action less damning." When someone is convicted of a crime, a lawyer will make a speech explaining why her client should receive a light punishment. This can be called *a speech in mitigation of sentence* and lawyers use the verb "to mitigate" to mean to make this speech.

❐

minuscule

Yes, so many people (including us) have misspelled the word (with an *i*) as "**miniscule**" that some dictionaries are accepting it. But **minuscule** deserves the proper spelling (with a *u*). It makes perfect sense when you realize it is derived from the Latin *minusculus* ("rather small, diminutive"). There is even a direct antonym: *majuscule,* from the Latin *majusculus* meaning "somewhat larger."

❑ A country depends on the heart of men: it is **minuscule** if the heart is small, and immense if the heart is great.—Simone Schwarz-Bart

❐

"Moslem" / Muslim / muslin (see also Islam / Islamic / Muslim)

The proper spelling is **Muslim**, not **Moslem**. The appellation *Mohammedan* (or *Muhammadan*) is not only archaic, but offensive.

❑ I am and always will be a **Muslim**. My religion is Islam.—Malcom X

Muslin is a plain-woven cotton fabric.

❑ **Muslin** can never be said to be wasted. I have heard my sister say so forty times, when she has been extravagant in buying more than she wanted, or careless in cutting it to pieces.—Jane Austen

❐

nauseous / nauseated / nauseating

This seems to be primarily an American problem. The English use *sick* to mean vomiting; when they are not feeling well they say they are *ill*. Americans say *sick* when they really mean *ill*. If everyone would just agree about *sick* and *ill* and, perhaps, use the word *queasy* on occasion—then we might skip this altogether.

You are on safe ground using **nauseated** ("caused to feel nausea") and **nauseating** ("causing to feel nausea"). If you are *nauseated,* it is because something else is *nauseating.* Simple.

The flap is over **nauseous**. Some feel *nauseous* should only be used to mean "causing nausea" and using it to mean "feeling sick to your stomach" is improper.

❑ Correct: *Putrescent zombies make us feel nauseated.*

It would be incorrect, however, upon seeing the putrescent zombies, to say:

❑ Incorrect: *Yuck. Zombies. I am nauseous.*

You should properly say:

❑ Correct: *Yuck. Zombies. I am nauseated.*

This makes a certain amount of sense. As someone named "Bremner" (sorry, we know nothing more about this source) allegedly said: "Just as one is poisoned by something poisonous, one is nauseated by something nauseous."

But we are so used to hearing *nauseous* used incorrectly, we might be misunderstood even when correct. For example:

❑ Correct: *Putrescent zombies are nauseous.*

This does NOT mean the zombies are feeling queasy. The zombies are causing queasiness, but it doesn't sound quite right.

American dictionaries are beginning to note that *nauseous* is not only commonly used to mean "feeling sick," it is now the *main* use. However, there is a bit of subtlety involved. As *Merriam-Webster* ["nauseous." *Merriam-Webster Online Dictionary.* 2003. http://www.merriam-webster.com (15 July 2003).] states:

⇨

Current evidence shows these facts: *nauseous* is most frequently used to mean physically affected with nausea, usually after a linking verb such as *feel* or *become;* figurative use is quite a bit less frequent. Use of *nauseous* in sense 1 [1: causing nausea or disgust: NAUSEATING] is much more often figurative than literal, and this use appears to be losing ground to *nauseating. Nauseated* is used more widely than *nauseous* in sense 2 [2: affected with nausea or disgust.]

In other words, when people use *nauseous* to mean "feeling physically sick," they tend to use it after a verb such as *feel, become,* or *get:*

❑ *I hope there are no more zombies because I'm getting nauseous.*

When people use it to mean "causing nausea", *nauseous* usually precedes a noun:

❑ *The nauseous odor of decaying flesh was ameliorated by burning incense.*

The older meaning of *nauseous,* both literal and figurative, is being reassigned to *nauseating:*

❑ *The zombie, with nauseating swiftness, scooped out the victim's brains.*

❑ *Meg looked a bit pale after her nauseating encounter with the zombies.*

We are, again, in the throes of language evolution. We hope such throes do not make you sick.

❒

naturism / naturist / naturalism/ naturalist

Naturism is another word for *nudism* and a **naturist** is a *nudist.*

❑ Organized **naturism** was called *Freikörperkultur* in Germany, the country of its origin. The **naturist** movement rapidly many adherents and became quite popular.

Naturalism describes the philosophical, theological, artistic, literary approach or style.

❑ The chief literary theorist on **naturalism** was Émile Zola

A **naturalist** can be one who believes in and follows the tenets of naturalism or someone knowledgeable about natural history, especially in zoology or botany.

❑ Charles Darwin was a British **naturalist** who became famous for his theories of evolution and natural selection.

❒

naval / navel

Naval has to do with the navy.

❑ Don't talk to me about **naval** tradition. It's nothing but rum, sodomy, and the lash.—Sir Winston Churchill

A **navel** is the depression in a belly marking the site of attachment of the umbilical cord.

❑ Thy **navel** is like a round goblet, which wanteth not liquor; thy belly is like a heap of wheat set about with lilies.—Song of Solomon 7:2

❐

nickel / "nickle"

The proper spelling, for both the metal and the U.S. coin, is **nickel**. The spelling "**nickle**" is now so rarely used that dictionaries often do not include it as a variant.

❑ A **nickel** ain't worth a dime anymore.—Yogi Berra

TANGENT: The Devil to Pay

Oddly enough, *nickel* means, more or less, "the Devil." Okay, so maybe it's more "less" than "more," but it's still interesting.

Nickel was not recognized as a separate metal until 1750 when miners in Saxony discovered what they, at first, thought was an unusual type of copper. This "new" metal was named *Kupfernickel,* "false copper," a combination of the German *Kupfer,* "copper," plus *Nickel,* "demon, rascal, goblin" (as in *Old Nick*). In 1751, the Swedish Baron Axel Frederik Cronstedt, in an attempt to obtain copper from *kopparnickel* (the Swedish language version of *Kupfernickel*), came up with a white metal instead. The baron, realizing it was not *koppar,* named the metal *nickel,* the other part of *kopparnickel/Kupfernickel* (now called *niccolite*).

The first U.S. coin to employ nickel was a 1-cent piece. First minted in 1856 the coin was almost 95% copper, but the small nickel content made it much lighter in color than previous all-copper cents. It was called both a "white cent" and a "nick." The first "nickel" 5-cent piece came along in 1866. The composition of the coin was 75% copper and 25% nickel. For four years during World War II, when nickel was a critical war material, nickels were 56% copper, 35% silver, and 9% manganese. After the war the coins returned to the 75%-25% mix and so remain. Yes, the nickel is only one quarter nickel.

❐

⚘ O ⚘

oar / or / ore

An **oar** is an implement used to row or steer a boat.

> ❑ There are some people who leave impressions not so lasting as the imprint of an **oar** upon the water.—Kate Chopin

Or is a conjunction used to indicate an alternative.

> ❑ Television is basically teaching whether you want it to **or** not.
> —Jim Henson

Ore is a mineral from which metal can be obtained

> ❑ Everything has its limit—iron **ore** cannot be educated into gold.
> —Mark Twain

❐

official / officious

Official relates to an authority or something authorized.

> ❑ Of the three **official** objects of our prison system: vengeance, deterrence, and reformation of the criminal, only one is achieved; and that is the one which is nakedly abominable.—George Bernard Shaw

Officious means "interfering in an annoyingly domineering way."

> ❑ No tyranny is so irksome as petty tyranny: the **officious** demands of policemen, government clerks, and electro-mechanical gadgets.
> —Edward Abbey

❐

OK / O.K. / okay

Okay is probably the single most recognized word on the planet, but there is no single "proper" spelling. The three shown above (no lower case abbreviations, no variant spelling) are all acceptable. Pick one and be consistent, but remember no matter how you spell it, *okay* is not considered acceptable in "formal" usage.

> ❑ It's **okay** to be a bad writer if you have something to say.—Bill Stott

❐

on / onto

When denoting action toward something, you can use either **on** or **onto**—but *onto* more specifically shows that the action started from somewhere else. Do you mean *Zelda bounced **on** the bed* or *Zelda bounced **onto** the bed? Scott ran **onto** the stage* means Scott was somewhere other than the stage when he started to run. *Scott ran **on** the stage* probably means Scott started running while already there.

❑ I had no idea of the character. But the moment I was dressed, the clothes and the make-up made me feel the person he was. I began to know him, and by the time I walked **onto** the stage he was fully born. —Charlie Chaplin

on to / onto

Sometimes **onto** and **on to** are interchangeable, but not always. Chances are you want to say: *Meet me by the gate, then we'll walk **on to** the lake* not *Meet me by the gate, then we'll walk **onto** the lake.* (The latter would require a miracle.)

On to is the adverb *on* followed by the preposition *to*. **Onto** is a single word (a compound preposition). If you mean "motion toward the upper surface of something" or "motion toward and then over"—use *onto: The Lone Ranger leapt **onto** Silver.* When *on* is an adverb, use *on to: Tonto rode **on to** the next town.*

Onto is also used colloquially to mean "aware of" or "know of": *She quickly caught **onto** his meaning. We knew we were **onto** something as soon as we solved the first clue.*

❑ A verbal art like poetry is reflective; it stops to think. Music is immediate, it goes **on to** become.—W.H. Auden

on / upon

On indicates position upon something; *on top of Old Smokey; put it **on** the table; post it **on** the board; wear it **on** your head; find it **on** page 47.* Those who take the "simplest is best" position feel *on* should almost always be used instead of **upon**. But, as Kenneth G. Wilson states in *The Columbia Guide to Standard American English* (1993), "[T]his is nonsense. Both are useful words, offering variety at the very least, and occasionally *upon* offers a precision *on* lacks or can usefully provide a slightly more elevated tone." Just make sure you know the difference between "elevated tone" and being pretentious.

❑ Chaos is the score **upon** which reality is written.—Henry V. Miller

oral / verbal

Even though **verbal** means "of, relating to, or consisting of words", most people use it to mean "spoken, not written." If you say you gave *verbal instructions*, you usually mean you have expressed those instructions with spoken words, otherwise you would probably have said you gave written orders. Technically, **to inform verbally** means **either** *spoken* or *written* communication; **to inform orally** means **only** *spoken communication.*

The Associated Press settles the matter of clarity by decreeing **oral** be used to refer to spoken words; **written** to refer to words put down on paper; **verbal** to *compare* words with other forms of communication. The *New York Times* uses **oral** for *spoken* and **verbal** for *spoken or written* words.

Oral also means "of or relating to used in or taken through the mouth." (See the entry **aural/oral** as well.)

❑ My opposition [to interviews] lies in the fact that offhand answers have little value or grace of expression, and that such **oral** give and take helps to perpetuate the decline of the English language.—James Thurber

❑ All really great lovers are articulate, and **verbal** seduction is the surest road to actual seduction.—Marya Mannes

❐

ordinance / ordnance

Ordinance is an authoritative decree, an act or ordering, or a law.

❑ Law is nothing other than a certain **ordinance** of reason for the common good, promulgated by the person who has the care of the community.—Thomas Aquinas

Ordnance refers to weapons and munitions.

❑ According to UNICEF there were approximately 3.5 million landmines and 350,000–800,000 tons of unexploded **ordnance** scattered throughout Viet Nam in 2000.

❐

orient / oriental / Oriental / "orientate"

Orient, as a noun, means "east." It is capitalized when referring to the region that includes Asia south and southeast of the Himalayas and the Malay archipelago west of the channel between Bali and Lombok. (*Bangkok is located in the Orient.*) The adjective form is **oriental** or **Oriental.** (*Oriental arborvitae is an Asiatic shrub.*)

❑ Our trouble is that we drink too much tea. I see in this the slow revenge of the **Orient,** which has diverted the Yellow River down our throats. —J.B. Priestley

Orient as a verb means "to find direction or give direction." The noun form of this kind of orienting is **orientation.**

❑ Every **orientation** presupposes a disorientation. —Hans Magnus Enzensberger

There is no such word as "**orientate.**" Folks probably confused and combined *orientation* and *oriented.* Nothing is "orientated" to anything; things are *oriented.*

❐

overdo / overdue

Overdo means "to do too much or go too far."

❑ Govern a great nation as you would cook a small fish. Do not **overdo** it.—Lao Tzu

Overdue means "past due; not paid at the scheduled time."

❑ The best of my education has come from the public library... my tuition fee is a bus fare and once in a while, five cents a day for an **overdue** book. You don't need to know very much to start with, if you know the way to the public library.—Lesley Conger

❐

❧ P ❧

pablum / Pablum / pabulum

In Latin **pabulum** means "food, fodder, nourishment." When introduced into English around 1730, it meant the same. By 1760 or so, it came to be used in the sense of stimulating intellectual nourishment (*pabulum cogitato* = "food for thought"). In 1930, three Canadian doctors at the Hospital for Sick Children in Toronto developed a bland infant cereal containing necessary minerals and vitamins for children's health. They named it **Pablum** (from the Latin word, *pabulum*). The name *Pablum* was eventually trademarked for the product. The pre-cooked dry infant cereal was nutritious and easy to prepare. It became so commonly used, the brand name came to be used to mean any infant cereal.

It is up to the trademark holder to protect a trademark from "general adoption as a generic term." When a trademark becomes part of common language, it can be declared generic. Trademark owners of names such as Coke, Kleenex, Popsicle, Band-Aid, and Jell-O are constantly fighting off such adoption. Words like aspirin, cellophane, nylon, thermos, and linoleum have already lost the battle. *Pablum* became a product of the Heinz food company in 1995 and the word remains trademarked.

However, after the baby food became well known, **pablum** was quickly adapted to mean:

> *Trite, insipid, or simplistic writing, speech, or conceptualization:* "We have to settle for the pablum that passes for the inside dope" *(Julie Salamon).*
> —from *American Heritage Dictionary of the English Language:* Fourth Edition. 2000.

According to the Associated Press, the *New York Times,* and others—the capitalized word means "bland baby food." Without a capital *p* it means "anything bland and oversimplified."

Remember that *pabulum* came to mean something that *nourishes* the mind more than two centuries ago. That is almost the opposite of what *pablum* means. But *Pablum* has only been around for about 70 years and *pablum* for less than that. Look the word *pabulum* up in many dictionaries and you'll find the meanings: 1. pablum; or 2. food, nourishment; or 3. both meanings: bland and oversimplified + nourishment.   ⇨

They are just as confused as we are. You may not find *pablum* in a dictionary at all, or only as part of the entry for *pabulum*. And, if you "spell check" *pablum* with some word processing software, you'll be told to change it to *pabulum*. Check the software's thesaurus, though, and there is no entry for either word.

It seems to us that **Pablum** has been genericized to **pablum** (meaning "insipid, simplistic ideas" or any "bland baby cereal"). If referring specifically to the Heinz product, then capitalize it. **Pabulum** should probably be ignored altogether unless using Latin. But that's just our thought.

❐

pail / pale

As an adjective, **pale** means, in general, "faint (color)" or "dim (light)."

> ❑ **Pale** death, with impartial step, knocks at the hut of the poor and the towers of kings.—Horace

Pale, as a noun, means "pointed piece of wood for fencing" and, by extension "boundary," thus the idiom **beyond the pale**. Anything *beyond the pale* is outside the boundaries, irrevocably unacceptable or completely unreasonable.

> ❑ Without one overt act of hostility, one upbraiding word, he contrived to impress me momently with the conviction that I was put **beyond the pale** of his favour.—Charlotte Brontë

A **pail** is a bucket.

> ❑ Education is not the filling of a **pail**, but the lighting of a fire.
> —William Butler Yeats

❐

palate / pallet / palette

The **palate** is the roof of the mouth. A person's **palate** is their ability to taste and judge good food and wine.

> ❑ I am prepared to believe that a dry martini slightly impairs the **palate**, but think what it does for the soul.—Alec Waugh

A **pallet** is a small bed or straw-filled mattress; a small portable platform for moving or storing cargo; or a hand tool with a flat blade used by potters for mixing and shaping clay.

> ❑ [Huck and Tom] found a small recess in the one nearest the base of the rock, with a **pallet** of blankets spread down in it; also an old suspender, some bacon rind, and the well-gnawed bones of two or three fowls.
> —Mark Twain

⇨

A **pallette** is an artist's board for mixing colors; a certain range of colors; or one of the rounded plates at the armpits of a suit of armor. In some cases you won't find **pallette** in a dictionary, and the first two meanings assigned to *pallet*. However, every usage authority and style book we consulted made the differentiation above.

> ❑ In our life there is a single color, as on an artist's **palette**, which provides the meaning of life and art. It is the color of love.—Marc Chagall

❐

parameter / perimeter

We already mentioned it might be wise to avoid *pabulum* altogether (see above). The same is true of **parameter.** Unless you are a scientist, programmer, or mathematician (or *very* confident you know what it means), you should probably use another word.

Perimeter means "the border or line around an object," especially a two-dimensional geometric figure. It has also come to refer to the border of any area or any kind of limit.

Originally a term in mathematics, **parameter** has several specific meanings in various scientific fields including astronomy and statistics. In mathematics, it boils down, more or less, to "a variable which has the same value in more than one equation."

Parameter has been used in the last 30 years or so to mean "a fixed boundary or a characteristic or defining element." Harry Shaw, in *Dictionary of Problem Words and Expressions*, called parameter a "fad word… constantly being misused by persons who apparently think it means 'limits' or 'perimeter' or 'boundary-line'." So, in an attempt to appear more scientific or technical, folks may find themselves considered as just the opposite.

There are plenty of other words (*border, boundary, criterion, factor, limit, scope,* etc.) that can be used with more precision and less pretension.

> ❑ [O]n the western **perimeter** of Europe lies the damp, demanding and obsessively interesting country called by its own people Cymru … and known to the rest of the world, if it is known at all, as Wales.
> —Jan Morris

> ❑ With four **parameters** you can model an elephant and with five you can make it wave its trunk but Walt Disney can make it fly.
> —Stephen Senn

❐

past / passed

Past refers to time, to events that happened before the present.

❑ He who controls the **past** commands the future. He who commands the future conquers the **past**.—George Orwell

Passed is an action, referring to someone or something passing.

❑ Books, like proverbs, receive their chief value from the stamp and esteem of the ages through which they have **passed**. —J. Paul Getty

A legal provision is *passed* and so is an exam. It's *passed* away, *passed* by, *passed* on, *passed* out, *passed* over, etc.

❐

peak / peek / pique

The noun **peak** means "the top of a mountain or something else high and pointed; the point of greatest development, value, or intensity." As a verb, **peak** means "to reach an uppermost point."

❑ I've been in on the beginning, the rise, **peak**, collapse and end of the talking picture.—Joseph L. Mankiewicz

A **peek** is a quick, possibly furtive glance. As a verb, **peek** means "to take a quick, furtive look."

❑ The only way for writers to meet is to share a quick **peek** over a common lamp-post.—Cyril Connolly

Pique comes from a French word meaning "a prick, irritation." In English, as a noun, it is a state of irritation caused by a perceived insult; resentment, offense taken (as in the cliché "fit of *pique*"). As a verb it can mean "to cause resentment or indignation" but, most commonly, it means "to provoke, arouse, or stimulate" (as in the cliché "*pique* someone's curiosity").

❑ How the imagination is **piqued** by anecdotes of some great man passing incognito, as a king in gray clothes.—Ralph Waldo Emerson

There is also a type of fabric called **piqué**. It is pronounced p-KAY.

❐

pedal / peddle / petal

The noun **pedal** means "a foot-operated lever." As a verb it means "move by means of pedals." A bicyclist is a **pedaler**.

The short, form-fitting slacks are called **pedal pushers** because bicyclists first wore them. You operate foot-operated levers to make music with a **pedal steel guitar** or the **pedal keyboard** of an organ. If you de-emphasize or play down something, you **soft-pedal** it.

❑ The **pedal** is the soul of the piano.—Anton Rubenstein

Peddle means "to sell." A **peddler** is someone who peddles goods. The meaning originally inferred that traveling was involved along with the selling. This seems to be shifting to use just selling without the "selling-by-traveling" inference.

❑ Their constant yelping about a free press means, with a few honorable exceptions, freedom to **peddle** scandal, crime, sex, sensationalism, hate, innuendo and the political and financial uses of propaganda. A newspaper is a business out to make money through advertising revenue. That is predicated on the circulation and you know what circulation depends on.—Raymond Chandler

A **petal** is a part of a flower.

❑ Writing a book of poetry is like dropping a rose **petal** down the Grand Canyon and waiting for the echo.—Don Marquis

perquisite / prerequisite

A **perquisite** is a payment, profit, special right, or privilege enjoyed as a result of ones position. The informal word **perk** is a shortening and alteration of *perquisite*.

❑ Assassination is the **perquisite** of princes.
—19th-century European court cliché

❑ Far too many executives have become more concerned with the "four P's"—pay, **perks**, power and prestige—rather than making profits for shareholders.—T. Boone Pickens

Prerequisite means "something that is required as a prior condition for something else" (noun). It can also be used as an adjective meaning "required as a prior condition."

❑ **Prerequisite** for rereadability in books: that they be forgettable.
—Jean Rostand

persecute / prosecute

Persecute means "to harass or pursue in order to cause suffering." The act of persecuting is **persecution.**

❏ However wicked men may be, they dare not profess themselves enemies to virtue; and when they wish to **persecute** it, they either call it false, or impute crimes to it.—François, Duc de la Rochefoucauld

Prosecute means "to pursue to the end, to accomplish; to bring legal action against someone." The act of prosecuting is **prosecution.** The side carrying out the legal claim is also referred to as **the prosecution.** An attorney representing the accuser (usually the government) is a **prosecutor.**

❏ An innocent man, if accused, can be acquitted; a guilty man, unless accused, cannot be condemned. It is, however, more advantageous to absolve an innocent than not to **prosecute** a guilty man.
—Marcus Tullius Cicero

❐

perspective / prospective

Perspective means "point of view, especially the ability to see the whole of something." In art, perspective is the method of representing the way objects appear smaller when they are further away and the way parallel lines appear to meet each other at a point in the distance.

❏ From the lowly **perspective** of a dog's eyes, everyone looks short.
—Chinese proverb

❏ A lustreless protrusive eye
Stares from the protozoic slime
At a **perspective** of Canaletto.
The smoky candle end of time
Declines.—T.S. Eliot

The adjective **prospective** means "concerned with or related to the future." Its noun form is **prospect.**

❏ American business long ago gave up on demanding that **prospective** employees be honest and hardworking. It has even stopped hoping for employees who are educated enough that they can tell the difference between the men's room and the women's room without having little pictures on the doors.—Dave Barry

❐

perspicuous / perspicacious

Perspicuous means "transparently clear; easily understandable."

❏ A mathematical proof must be **perspicuous.**—Ludwig Wittgenstein

Perspicacious means "mentally acute, insightful; penetratingly discerning."

❏ Written by Hunter S. Thompson as he experienced it in 1971, it balances the nonsensical ramblings of a rug-addled lunatic with the **perspicacious** wisdom of one of the twentieth century's most eloquent writers.—Back Cover of *Fear and Loathing in Las Vegas*

poor / pore / pour

Poor means "lacking money or the means for an adequate or comfortable life; unsatisfactory: low in degree or quality; deserving of pity."

❏ The **poor** are always ragged and dirty, in very picturesque clothes, and on their **poor** shoes lies the earth of the Lacustrine period. And yet what a privilege it is to be even a beggar in Rome!—M.E.W. Sherwood

The verb **pore** means "to read or study intently." It is usually (but not always, as our somewhat archaic example below shows) followed by the word *over*.

❏ Mistresses are like books; if you **pore** upon them too much, they dose you and make you unfit for company; but if used discreetly, you are the fitter for conversation by 'em.—William Wycherley

The noun **pore** means "a very small hole in the skin or on the surface."

❏ He that has eyes to see and ears to hear may convince himself that no mortal can keep a secret. If his lips are silent, he chatters with his fingertips; betrayal oozes out of him at every **pore.**—Sigmund Freud

Pour means "to flow in a continuous stream."

❏ If you **pour** oil and vinegar into the same vessel, you would call them not friends but opponents.—Aeschylus

prescribe / proscribe

Prescribe means "recommend with authority" or "to issue a medical prescription."

❏ The free way of life proposes ends, but it does not **prescribe** means.
—Robert F. Kennedy

Proscribe means "to condemn or forbid."

❏ When a legislature undertakes to **proscribe** the exercise of a citizen's constitutional rights it acts lawlessly and the citizen can take matters into his own hands and proceed on the basis that such a law is no law at all.—William O. Douglas

❐

principal / principle

Principal means "first in order of importance; main." (*Principals* head schools.)

❏ The **principal** rule of art is to please and to move. All the other rules were created to achieve this first one.—Jean Racine

Principle means a basis of a system of thought or belief

❏ The first **principle** of a free society is an untrammeled flow of words in an open forum.—Adlai Stevenson

❐

prophecy / prophesy

Prophecy (final syllable pronounced *see*) is a noun referring to a prediction of the future or to a divinely inspired revelation.

❏ I see Macbeth as a young, open-faced warrior, who is grad-ually sucked into a whirlpool of events because of his ambition. When he meets the weird sisters and hears their **prophecy**, he's like the man who hopes to win a million—a gambler for high stakes.—Roman Polanski

Prophesy (final syllable pronounced *sigh*) is a verb that means "predicting or delivering a prophetic vision."

❏ I always avoid **prophesying** beforehand, because it is a much better policy to **prophesy** after the event has already taken place.
—Sir Winston Churchill

❐

prostate / prostrate

Prostate is the gland found in males.

- ❏ Since I came to the White House I got two hearing aids, a colon operation, skin cancer, a **prostate** operation and I was shot. The damn thing is, I've never felt better in my life.—Ronald Reagan

Prostrate refers to lying face down.

- ❏ The French at heart are monarchists. They like to **prostrate** themselves in front of the monarch, whom they now call president, and every seven years or so they guillotine him.—Hervé de Charette

❐

proposal / proposition

We often see these two nouns used interchangeably, but most authorities make a distinction in meaning between the two. Just what that difference is, however, depends on the authority.

Like *propose* and *propound,* both **proposal** and **proposition** come from the Latin verb *proponere,* "to set forth." As nouns, both mean "something put forth; a suggestion or assumption; an offer of some sort."

Definitions for *proposition* tend toward the meaning "a suggestion offered for consideration or discussion." It can also be loosely used to mean "any concern or matter."

A *proposal* seems to be a more definite offer or plan, perhaps one put in writing. We've even seen it suggested that there is an order involved: A *proposition* is made. If accepted, *proposals* are made that will complete the transaction. There are additional specific meanings for *proposal* as well. In mathematics, for instance, a *proposal* is a statement that is to be proved. In philosophy it is a formal statement that is capable of being judged true or false.

- ❏ You can get assent to almost any **proposition** so long as you are not going to do anything about it.—Nathaniel Hawthorne

- ❏ Controversial **proposals,** once accepted, soon become hallowed. —Dean Acheson

Proposal and *proposition* have more easily distinguishable meanings when it comes to personal interactions. A *proposal* is an offer of marriage; a *proposition* is an invitation to have sex without benefit of that socially and legally sanctioned union. In this latter sense, *proposition* is also a verb meaning "to make such offer."

❐

quash / squash

The verb **quash** usually means "to put down completely with force or intimidation; to invalidate."

> ❏ Ever since September 11 President George W. Bush and Attorney General John Ashcroft have tried to **quash** dissent by questioning the patriotism of people who seek to protect our civil rights and liberties. —Unsigned Editorial, *San Francisco Chronicle* (4 July 2002)

The verb **squash** means "to violently compress out of natural shape or condition."

> ❏ Silicon Valley is like a person running around in front of a steamroller. You can outrun the steamroller on any given day. But if you ever sit down you get **squashed**.—Bob Boschert

---

TANGENT: The Difference Between Squash & Squash

You learned (above) that the verbs *quash* and *squash* do not mean the same thing. Both come, more or less, through Old French and from the same Latin source. There are also several noun versions of *squash*. The two most common are the *game of squash* and *the gourd, fruit and/or vine called squash*. Students at England's Harrow school invented the game of *squash* around 1830. They took a punctured ball from a game called *rackets* and discovered it "squashed" when it hit a wall and the rest is history. THAT *squash* is basically the same word as the verb above. The *squash* you might grow in your garden has, however, nothing etymologically to do with the other *squash* words. It comes from Anglo alteration of the Narragansett Indian word *askútasquash*. *Asq* means "raw, un-cooked" and *-ash* is a plural ending for the inanimate noun *askutasq*, so you'll find this variously translated as "green things eaten green" or "green things eaten raw" or "young things eaten raw" or just "eaten uncooked." We're not sure of the exact translation, but we know it has nothing to do with Latin or Old French.

---

quote / quotation / quotation marks

Quote is a verb that means "to repeat the words of a writer or speaker."

❑ When I **quote** others I do so in order to express my own ideas more clearly.—Michel de Montaigne

Quotation is a noun referring to the words quoted or the act of quoting. It also has a specialized meaning of "the current price of a commodity, stock, or security." *(Investors can access real-time stock quotes online.)* This meaning has been extended to include any formal price. *(The company provided a quote on car insurance for us.)*

❑ He wrapped himself in **quotations**—as a beggar would enfold himself in the purple of Emperors.—Rudyard Kipling

Quotation marks are the punctuation marks used to enclose a *quotation.*

❑ It is an old error of man to forget to put **quotation marks** where he borrows from a woman's brain!—Anna Garlin Spencer

Quotation has been colloquially shortened to **quote** and applied to the meanings above. **Quotes,** plural, is used to mean *quotation marks,* as is *quote mark(s). (He needs to put quotes around his story's dialogue.)*

TANGENT: Quoth the Mavens

According to *The American Heritage Book of English Usage* (1996) and other authorities, the noun *quote* has been used as a truncation of *quotation* for more than a century and its informal use is widespread. [A relatively recent application of *quote* is in word processing software that offers you a choice of straight (or dumb) *quotes* and curly (or smart) quotes.] Experts (and we*) particularly dislike the use of *quote* as a synonym for "dictum or saying," as in "Quotes from Mao, Castro, and Che Guevara... are as germane to our highly technological, computerized society as a stagecoach on a jet runway at Kennedy Airport." (Saul Alinsky) Try always to avoid this use in writing and, in formal situations, steer clear of using *quote* when you mean *quotation.*

—⁓—

*Yes, we realize that on the Writers On the Net Web site, we use the word *quotes* instead of the word *quotations.* We know it is improper, but five letters fit the menu better than ten. This is no excuse, but we are divided equally between those who feel guilty and punish ourselves daily for this lapse over which they have no control and those who feel the first half should chill.

✣R✣

rack / wrack

There are many words spelled **rack**. Two of them are variants of words spelled **wrack**. (We never said English made sense.) We'll skip over the noun *rack* with the meanings "a rib section of meat (as in *rack of lamb*)," "high clouds," "the bar that fits into a pinion," "antlers," "rapid gait of a horse," and some others. That brings us to *rack* meaning "a framework or stand for holding or displaying things: a clothes rack, a book rack, a hat rack, etc."

❑ Girls need to prove their love like a moose needs a hat **rack**.
—Abigail Van Buren

Back in the not-so-good old days, there existed an engine of torture called a *rack*. This frame was used to stretch, disjoint, or mutilate victims. Obviously this was painful, so a figurative meaning was derived that is synonymous with *pain*.

❑ In old days men had the **rack**. Now they have the Press.—Oscar Wilde

Rack also has quite a few interesting verb meanings ("to drain from the dregs," "what you do to billiard balls," "to run or fly in a high wind," etc.). We'll (again) stick to torture. The verb *rack* means "to torment on a rack" or, more commonly nowadays, "to cause physical or mental torment."

❑ You and me, we sweat and strain
Body all achin' and **racked** with pain
Tote that barge and lift that bail
You get a little drunk and you lands in jail.—Jerome Kern

This verb appears in *nerve-racking* and the phrase *rack one's brains.*

❑ Go, my songs, to the lonely and the unsatisfied,
Go also to the **nerve-racked**, go to the enslaved-by-convention,
Bear to them my contempt for their oppressors.—Ezra Pound

❑ And the fire I feel for the woman I love is driving me insane
Knowing she's waiting and I just can't get there
Lord only knows that I've **racked my brain**
To try and find a way to see that woman in old Mexico—Hoyt Axton

⇨

Some consider **wrack** as two different nouns: one meaning "destruction or ruin" (as in *wrack and ruin*) the other meaning "wreckage." Those meanings are so close, many (including us) settle for *wrack* to generally mean, either literally or figuratively, "destruction" OR "wreckage." Further senses include "a wrecked ship" and "marine vegetation cast up on shore by the sea." The verb *wrack* usually means "to forcefully smash or wreck."

This would all be much easier if *wrack* did not have *rack*-with-no-*w* as an acceptable alternative spelling. Thus: *Enron was racked by the disclosures.* Does this mean the company was suffering (metaphorically) from pain or is it ruined? It's probably both, but we really can't determine if it is one or the other from the sentence. Make it *Enron was wracked by the disclosures* and chances are it means the company was smashed all to hell. The *rack* that is synonymous with "pain," does not normally have *wrack* as an acceptable variant.

Perspicacious readers will probably notice a spineless lack of definitive opinion in the two paragraphs above. We know. There is no infallible, final decision in many of these matters.

❒

rain / reign / rein

Rain is precipitation.

- ❑ The **rain** in Spain stays mainly in the plain.—Alan Jay Lerner

Rain can also mean "fall in a large amount."

- ❑ But the day Lot left Sodom, fire and sulfur **rained** down from heaven and destroyed them all.—Luke 17:29

Rain can also refer to anything happening rapidly or in quick successive bursts.

- ❑ Helmet and shield rang out as the great stones **rained** upon them... —Homer

Reign means "to rule" or "a period of domination by someone or something powerful."

- ❑ The **reign** of imagology begins where history ends.—Milan Kundera

A **rein** is a strap for controlling an animal.

- ❑ When a horse comes to the edge of the cliff, it is too late to draw **rein**; when a boat reaches midstream, it is too late to stop the leaks. —Chinese proverb

The idiom is **free rein** NOT "free reign."

- ❑ Keep your passions in check, but beware of giving your reason **free rein**.—Karl Kraus

❒

raise / rise

Raise means "to grow or cultivate; to cause to lift or to lift something."

❑ Being sixty-five... became a crossroads. We said, "We have nothing to lose, so we can **raise** hell."—Maggie Kuhn

Rise means "to ascend, move upward, or to assume an upright position (especially from lying, kneeling, or sitting); to return from death." As a verb, *rise* means an "increase."

❑ Early to **rise** and early to bed makes a male healthy and wealthy and dead.—James Thurber

❑

rap / wrap

Rap is a little word with many meanings. *Rap* (probably imitating the sound made) started out (around 1300) to mean "a serious blow with a weapon," but quickly came to mean "a quick, light blow." By extension it came to mean "knock or tap sharply." There is, of course, a verb form:

❑ While I nodded, nearly napping, suddenly there came a tapping,
As of some one gently **rapping, rapping** at my chamber door.
"'Tis some visitor," I muttered, "tapping at my chamber door—
Only this, and nothing more."—Edgar Allan Poe

To *rap (someone's) knuckles* ("give light punishment") is first found in 1749. The meaning of "rebuke or blame" was introduced in 1777. Slang for criminal accusation (as in *bum rap*, a false charge) was in print by 1903. This colloquial use was slightly varied for idioms like *beat the rap* ("escape punishment, specifically a sentence to prison"); *to get the rap* ("to receive blame or be scolded"); *pin (hang, tie) the rap on* ["to charge (a suspect), proving the validity (perhaps falsely) with circumstantial evidence"]; *take the rap*, (accept responsibility and its consequences).

Sometime before 1880 *rap* became a British slang term meaning "say, utter." This may be where the verb *rap*, meaning "to talk informally," originated. (Even Winston Churchill is known to have used *rap* in this manner in 1933.) It eventually came to mean "informally discuss or debate" in the African-American community and this meaning was well-established by the mid-1960s. One additional meaning of *rap* was "a special banter used by a young man to convince a young woman to grant him sexual favors." Boastful repartee and put-downs among young men was also dubbed as *rap*. (The oral tradition of African cultures—and the necessity of oral tradition due to the slavery system—has always been an essential element of black American culture.) In the early 1970s emceeing was the form of verbal expression of New York City hip-hop culture

⇨

(the other components were graffiti art, break dancing, and dj cutting and scratching). This ability to rhyme on beat and execute clever word play and metaphors came to be called *rap*. In the fall of 1979, the Sugarhill Gang's recording *Rapper's Delight* established *rap* as a word in mainstream culture.

❑ There's no such thing as **rap** music. *Rap* is rhyming lyrical form over any kind of music. So long as there are different types of music, *rap* will always be around. Besides, there will always be people that can't sing. —Fresh Prince [Will Smith]

The word **wrap** has nothing to do with any of those definitions of *rap*. Even its origins are different. *Wrap* as a noun can mean "a piece of clothing tied around the body, a jacket, or long piece of cloth which a woman wears around her shoulders." It is also material which is used to cover or protect objects. The completion of a schedule or session for filming or videotaping is also termed *a wrap*.

❑ If you are going especially for a ball, but not given by your hostess, needless to say, you take a ball dress and an evening **wrap**. In the autumn or winter, a fur coat will do double service for coat and **wrap**. —Emily Post

❑ Trash from gift **wrap** and shopping bags totals about 4 million tons each year.

As a verb, *wrap* means "to arrange or fold as a cover or protection; twine or coil around; enclose or enfold completely with or as if with a covering.

❑ I cannot forecast to you the action of Russia. It is a riddle **wrapped** in a mystery inside an enigma.—Sir Winston Churchill

The phrase **wrap up** means "to bring to a conclusion, settle finally or successfully; to summarize or recapitulate."

❑ **Wrap up** the 20th century; Fred Astaire is gone.— Jack Kroll

The idioms **under wraps** and **wrapped up in** are also frequently used. To **put** (or keep) **something under wraps** is to conceal it.

❑ Baseball is a game, yes. It is also a business. But what is most truly is disguised combat. For all its gentility, its al-most leisurely pace, baseball is violence under **wraps**.—Willie Mays

If you are completely immersed or absorbed in something you're **wrapped up in** it.

❑ A man **wrapped up in** himself makes a very small bundle. —Benjamin Franklin

ravage / ravish

Ravage means "to devastate, ruin, destroy."

❑ The world has suffered more from the **ravages** of ill-advised marriages than from virginity.—Ambrose Bierce

Ravish means "to rape or to violently capture and abduct." It can also be used in the figurative sense to mean "overcome with emotion, transported with delight."

❑ He in a few minutes **ravished** this fair creature, or at least would have **ravished** her, if she had not, by a timely compliance, prevented him. —Henry Fielding

❑ The green trees when I saw them first through one of the gates transported and **ravished** me, their sweetness and unusual beauty made my heart to leap, and almost mad with ecstasy, they were such strange and wonderful things.—Thomas Traherne

Yes, we admit both *ravage* and *ravish* are synonymous in one sense: "to seize or rob and carry off." The Associated Press feels that only *people* can be *ravished*. Avoid confusion. Use *ravage* when destroying and devastating and, if carrying things off, then plunder, pillage, or take spoils, too.

❐

reek / wreak / wreck

Reek, as a noun, means "a strong offensive odor; a stench; or vapor, steam, or smoke." *(The fire died out and left the ruins reeking.)*

❑ Let me feel thee again, old sea! let me leap into thy saddle once more. I am sick of these terra firma toils and cares; sick of the dust and **reek** of towns.—Herman Melville

As a verb, **reek** means "to emit or be pervaded by something unpleasant; to give off smoke, fumes, warm vapor, steam, etc." It sometimes is used synonymously with *smack*, meaning to have an element suggestive (of something).

❑ The present **reeks** of mediocrity and the atom bomb.—René Magritte

The meanings related to *vapor, steam, smoke*, etc. seem to be disappearing, although that connotation was the original. (As in *The fire died out and left the ruins reeking.*) Knowing this definition, however, helps make sense of literature in which *reek* refers to *persons or animals in a heated and perspiring state* [Harriet Beecher Stowe in *Uncle Tom's Cabin* (1852): "Sam appeared...with Haley's horse by his side, reeking with sweat"] or of blood freshly shed or smeared with that blood [Edward Hyde, Earl Claredon (1674): "Whilst these perfidious wretches had their hands still reeking in the precious blood of their sovereign."].

⇨

Now, knowing all this, if you read of a *warrior reeking with the blood of a slain enemy,* you can envision a scene of a sweating dude smeared with steaming blood instead of just thinking the phrase means he smelled bad because of some blood on him.

Wreak is also pronounced *reek.* You usually hear it in the phrase *wreak havoc.* The phrase *wreak havoc,* by the way, was first used by Agatha Christie in 1923 according to *Take Our Word for It,* Issue 48 (3 August 1999).

Wreak in this sense of *bringing about, causing* is often confused with **wreck**, which means "to ruin by or as if by violence" (verb) and (noun) "the action of wrecking; the fact or state of being wrecked; or the ruins left by wreaking." **Wreaking** destruction may leave a *wreck.* Storms, unruly children, invading armies, pollutants, and the like *wreak havoc* they do not *wreck* it.

Wreaked is the past tense and past participle of *wreak.* Some folks are under the impression that **wrought** is the past tense and past participle of *wreak*—it's not. *Wrought* is a past tense and past participle of *work* (although *worked* is now more commonly used than *wrought*).

The phrase *work havoc* is perfectly acceptable, so you could have *wrought havoc* or *worked havoc.* Many will think, though, that *wrought havoc* is a mistake for *wreaked havoc.* To avoid having to deal with these people it is best to skip this phrase altogether.

❒

regardless / "irregardless"

Wondering why this entry is listed under *r* rather than *i?* Linguistic purists don't consider **irregardless** a word at all. How could we alphabetize by something that doesn't exist?

Despite this, we are impure and permissive and do not deny it is a word; *irregardless* is frequently used in common speech. It's a ridiculous double negative and definitely substandard, but we aren't going refuse that it exists. We advise against using it in your writing and mention that its use in speech may cause snickering and dismay in some circles.

❑ Hope is definitely not the same thing as optimism. It is not the conviction that something will turn out well, but the certainty that something makes sense, **regardless** of how it turns out.—Václav Havel

❒

retch / wretch

Retch means "to vomit or to suffer involuntary spasms of ineffectual vomiting."

- ❑ In the plot, people came to the land; the land loved them; they worked and struggled and had lots of children. There was a Frenchman who talked funny and a greenhorn from England who was a fancy-pants but when it came to the crunch he was all courage. Those novels would make you **retch.**—Robertson Davies

A **wretch** is a pitiful miserable person or a base, despicable, vile person

- ❑ A needy, hollow-eyed, sharp-looking **wretch,**
  A living-dead man.—William Shakespeare

❒

riffle / rifle

The noun **rifle** means "the shoulder weapon with a long barrel and a rifled bore."

- ❑ A quotation in a speech, article or book is like a **rifle** in the hands of an infantryman. It speaks with authority.—Brendan Francis

What's a "rifled bore"? (No, it is not a tedious person who has been shot with a rifle.) To rifle a bore (the inner surface of a hollow cylindrical object) you cut spiral grooves into it. The flat surfaces of the barrel between the grooves are called the *lands.* The distance (in hundredths of an inch or in millimeters) between opposite lands determines the caliber of a weapon. A 38-caliber weapon has a distance of .38 inches from the top edge of one land to the top edge of a land on the opposite side. With the exception of smooth-bored shotguns, all firearms have "rifled" barrels that are unique to a particular manufacturer. Comparison of a bullet found at a crime scene (or in a victim) with a bullet fired (into a water tank) from a suspected gun will show (via the characteristic lands, grooves, twist) if the manufacturer, model, caliber, and sometimes even year of make are the same. Since no two barrels have identical striation patterns, further examination of striations on a bullet can match it exactly to a particular gun.

Otherwise, as a verb **rifle** usually means "to search through someone's belongings in an unauthorized way."

- ❑ [Viewing] Robert Mulligan's...beautifully choreographed, ultrastylized opening credits, featuring a tight focus on random objects in a keepsake box **rifled** through by childish hands, is like watching the birth of contemporary filmmaking.—Adele Marley

⇨

Riffle can mean "a showy way to shuffle that involves flicking the edges of the playing cards." You can also *riffle* through a magazine or book by flicking through the pages.

❏ To bring a pack of perfectly ordered playing cards close to random takes, if you use the **riffle** shuffle, only seven shuffles according to Professor Persi Diaconis of Harvard.

❐

right / rite / wright / write

There once was a writer named Wright
who instructed his son to write right.
He said, 'son' write Wright right.
It's not right to write Wright as "rite"—
try to write Wright all right!

We know of about a dozen meanings for **right** as an adjective, another dozen as a noun, and yet another dozen as an adverb. There are at least three verb meanings and quite a few common idioms. In brief, we'll cover it with the meanings "just; correct; something legally or morally due; opposite of 'left'" and remind you this is not a dictionary.

❏ Always do the **right** thing. This will gratify some people and astonish the rest.—Mark Twain

A **rite** is a ritual or ceremony.

❏ My rule of life prescribed as an absolutely sacred **rite** smoking cigars and also the drinking of alcohol before, after and if need be during all meals and in the intervals between them.—Sir Winston Churchill

A **wright** is an artisan, a skilled worker (usually used in combination: *shipwright, playwright, wheelwright*).

❏ A play has two authors, the **playwright** and the actor. —Eric Bentley

To **write** is to record in writing

❏ I wish I could **write** as mysterious as a cat.—Edgar Allan Poe

Although a person who writes plays is a **playwright**, a person who writes screenplays is a **screenwriter**.

The legal protection of a creation is **copyright** NOT "copywrite."

A **copywriter** writes advertising or publicity copy.

❐

role / rôle / roll

Role means "position or function" or "a character or a part in a theatrical work." (You'll sometimes find this second meaning spelled **rôle**, with the French circumflex accent. We suspect this is a rather pretentious spelling unless you are writing in French.)

❏ Man's **role** is uncertain, undefined, and perhaps unnecessary. —Margaret Mead

❏ If you have to be in a soap opera try not to get the worst **role**. —Judy Garland

Roll has many meanings:

○ Move.

❏ A barrel full of certainties won't **roll** very far.—Gerd de Ley

○ Piece of bread.

❏ Three meals of thin gruel a day, with an onion twice a week, and half a **roll** on Saturdays.—Charles Dickens

○ List of names.

❏ When they call the **roll** in the Senate, the Senators do not know whether to answer "Present" or "Not guilty."—Theodore Roosevelt

○ The act of throwing dice

❏ God's dice always have a lucky **roll**.—Sophocles

○ Make something flat.

❏ Once a new technology **rolls** over you, if you're not part of the steamroller, you're part of the road.—Stewart Brand

○ Shape by rolling.

❏ To say yes, you have to sweat and **roll** up your sleeves and plunge both hands into life up to the elbows. It is easy to say no, even if saying no means death.—Jean Anouilh

○ A continuous repeated sound.

❏ I have a simple life. I mean, you just give me a drum **roll**, they announce my name, and I come out and sing. In my job I have a contract that says I'm a singer. So I sing.—Tony Bennett

—and many more. It is also used in many phrases (*anti-roll bar, egg roll, heads will roll, let's roll, on a roll, rock'n'roll, roll call,* etc.)

❏ **Roll** over, Beethoven,
And tell Tchaikovsky the news.—Chuck Berry

❒

root / (en) route / route / rout

A **root** is the underground part of a plant that obtains water and food and holds the plant firm in the ground. From this basic meaning come many others, most having to do with origins, source, basics, and fundamentals. As a verb, a sow can *root* (poke with her snout) for truffles and we can *root* (cheer on) for the pig to find the truffles. (At around $500 per pound we can be quite enthusiastic about finding truffles.)

❑ Ignorance, the **root** and stem of all evil.—Plato

The phrase **en route** is French for "on the way (to)" or "along the way," but it is now fully adopted into English. (A few other examples of anglicized French words are: *argot, detente, entourage, poseur, riposte,* and *soiree.* You might also want to see the *Tangent* on page 52.) It is pronounced *en ROOT* or *ahn ROOT,* or (if you are good at nasalizing French vowels), *awng ROOT.* (Do not pronounce this *route* to rhyme with *out.*) Common errors in usage include spelling *en* as *on,* and spelling as one word.

❑ Amelia Earhart's plane disappeared on 2 July 2 1937 while **en route** from Lae, New Guinea, to Howland Island.

A **rout** is an overwhelming defeat. (Pronounced just as spelled.)

❑ Spent. Wench, whiskey and tail-end
Of your overseas disease
Rot and **rout** you by degrees.—Gwendolyn Brooks

A **route** is a regularly followed path, road, or an established line of travel. Do you pronounce it *root* or *rout?* We found sources acknowledging both or claiming one was correct and the other incorrect. We'll leave it up to you.

❑ I was too old for a paper **route,** too young for Social Security and too tired for an affair.—Erma Bombeck

❐

rote / wrote

Rote means "memorization by repetition."

❑ Sciences may be learned by **rote,** but wisdom not.—Laurence Sterne

Wrote is the past tense of *write*

❑ Thurber did not write the way a surgeon operates, he **wrote** the way a child skips rope, the way a mouse waltzes.—E.B. White

❐

sacrilege / sacrilegious

Watch the spelling of these two words, especially the vowels in the second and third syllables of both. They are neither etymologically related to nor spelled like *religion* or *religious*. *Sacrilege* came from the Latin *sace* ("sacred") plus *leger* ("to gather or steal"). Its base meaning, then, is "the stealing of sacred things." The *OED* shrinks from committing to a specific etymology for *religion*, but John Ayto ties it to *religio* (Latin for "obligation" or "bond"). Other etymologists usually acknowledge this explanation.

❑ The new always carries with it the sense of violation, of **sacrilege**. What is dead is sacred; what is new, that is different, is evil, dangerous, or subversive.—Henry Miller

❑ A singer starts by having his instrument as a gift from God... When you have been given something in a moment of grace, it is **sacrilegious** to be greedy.—Marian Anderson

❐

sail / sale

The meanings of **sail** are connected to the large piece of fabric that catches the wind on a boat.

❑ I have seen old ships **sail** like swans asleep—James Elroy Flecker

The meanings of **sale** are connected to transfer of ownership for a price.

❑ If you want to buy my wares
Follow me and climb the stairs.
Love for **sale**.—Cole Porter

❐

sanction

Sanction, as a verb, means *both* "to give permission" and "to punish or penalize." As a noun, it means *both* "permission, authorization, or support" and "penalty" or "coercive measure by several nations acting together against a nation violating international law." Words that have two opposite meanings are known as *contronym*s or *antagonym*s. Other examples include ravel ("to disentangle" and "to tangle") and buckle ("fasten together" and "fall apart"). Make sure your context clarifies your meaning.

- ❑ Evil requires the **sanction** of the victim.—Ayn Rand

- ❑ [The imposition of capital punishment for the crime of murder] is an extreme **sanction** suitable to the most extreme of crimes.—Potter Stewart

❒

sanguine / sanguinary

If you are **sanguine,** you are a jolly optimistic sort and might have a ruddy complexion. If you have a **sanguinary** nature, however, you are bloodthirsty and murderous.

How did this huge disparity of definitions occur? Both words go back to the Latin word for blood, *sang* [as does *sangfroid* ("cool blood") from French *sang* "blood" + *froid* "cold" and *sangria* ("a red wine-based punch") from Spanish for "bleeding."]

Ancient Greek medicine contended that, to remain healthy, four bodily fluids had to be kept in balance. This theory became the foundation of medical knowledge in Western civilization. In the Middle Ages, the word *humor* was used to connote these fluids. (*Humor* comes from the Latin *umor* meaning "liquid" or "fluid.") Humors determined not only physical health, but disposition as well. The *sanguine* humor was associated with blood. A small excess of blood made a person *sanguine*: red-cheeked, vital, and joyful. *Sanguine* came to mean "cheerful, optimistic, confident." *Sanguine* also meant (and means) a *blood-red color*. (See the *Tangent* below for more about *Bloodletting, Barbers, and Balance*.)

Sanguinary, by a somewhat different route, came to mean "bloody, bloodthirsty, or bloodstained" and by extension "grim, cruel, murderous."

Thus, when Abraham Lincoln wrote in a letter: "Still let us not be over-*sanguine* of a speedy final triumph [in what would come to be known as the U.S. Civil War]. Let us be quite sober" he meant we should not be too optimistic in hoping for a quick end. And when Ulysses S. Grant wrote in his *Personal Memoirs* that nations "like individuals, are punished for their transgressions. We got our punishment in the most *sanguinary* and expensive war of modern times" he was referring to the extremely bloody, murderous nature of that war.

⇨

TANGENT: Bloodletting, Barbers & Balance

The three humors, other than *sanguine,* were *phlegm, yellow bile,* and *black bile.* To restore health a balance was achieved through purging, starving, vomiting or, in the case of the sanguine humor—bloodletting. From the early 13th century into the 18th century, barbers commonly performed bloodletting, along with dental extractions, minor surgeries, and sometimes amputations. Barbers often advertised their craft with a red (for blood) and white (for tourniquet or bandage) striped pole. The pole represented the stick squeezed by the patient to dilate the veins.

This association of barbers and surgery came about after the Fourth Lateran Council (1215). Roman Catholic priests had become de facto doctors as the Roman Empire dissolved. Monasteries housed what hospitals there were as well as the knowledge of earlier medical practices.

One of the 70 canons presented by Pope Innocent III and approved by the council decreed that priests, deacons, and subdeacons were forbidden to perform surgical operations.

Since barbers were accustomed to using razors, it was presumed that they would be skillful in intentionally cutting the skin, so they were taught bloodletting. Barber surgery continued until the mid-18th century.

Once the physicians were in charge, bloodletting reached its zenith in the 18th and early 19th centuries. The draining of 16-30 ounces (one to four pints) of blood was typical. It took until the end of the 19th century (1875–1900) for bloodletting to be considering quackery.

❐

set / sit

Set means "to place something somewhere." Concrete *sets,* the sun *sets,* you *set* a table or a date, you *set* out to conquer, you *set* about to do something, *set* the time on your clock, *set* someone up to take a fall, *set* forth to accomplish, you *set* something in motion...

❏ Do I dare **set** forth here the most important, the most useful rule of all education? It is not to save time, but to squander it.—Jean-Jacques Rousseau

Sit means "to be seated." Judges *sit* on benches, in England you *sit* for exams, you *sit* out a game, you *sit* up all night, you shouldn't *sit* in judgment of others, but you should *sit* at the feet of someone you admire, you *sit* on your backside or *sit* on your hands and do nothing, you *sit* in on meetings and *sit* in for someone who is absent, you *sit* down, *sit* tight, *sit* pretty, and *sit* under...

❏ We **sit** in the mud...and reach for the stars.—Ivan Sergeyevich Turgenev

Got the idea? Unless you want to intentionally use a rural dialect—as the invitation in *The Ballad of Jed Clampitt* is for "y'all" to "set a spell"—people *sit,* even for a spell. Hens, however, may *sit* or *set* on their eggs.

❐

sew / so / sow

Sew means "to stich."

❏ If you like to make things out of wood, or **sew**, or dance, or style people's hair, or dream up stories and act them out, or play the trumpet, or jump rope, or whatever you really love to do, and you love that in front of your children, that's going to be a far more important gift than anything you could ever give them wrapped up in a box with ribbons. —Fred M. Rogers

So is an adverb generally meaning "in order that, in such a manner, or very much."

❏ It's not that I'm **so** smart, it's just that I stay with problems longer. —Albert Einstein

Sow (pronounced to rhyme with *low*) means to plant seeds.

❏ When men **sow** the wind it is rational to expect that they will reap the whirlwind.—Frederick Douglass

When *sow* is pronounced to rhyme with *now*, it means a female hog.

❒

shear / sheer

Shear means "to remove by cutting or clipping." *Shears* are a sharp cutting instrument.

❏ It is the part of a good shepherd to **shear** his flock, not to skin it. —Latin proverb

Wind shear is a technical term that is now often used to refer to a change in wind speed or direction, or both, over a short distance. **Wind shear** can be both vertical and horizontal and can cause anything from minor turbulence to tornadoes.

Sheer, as a verb, can mean "to swerve, to veer away." As an adjective it can mean:

○ Wholly obvious, pure, clear, utter, total, undiluted.

○ Very steep or perpendicular.

○ Transparent, see-through.

❏ The basis of optimism is **sheer** terror.—Oscar Wilde

The idiom **sheer ice** probably refers to *pure ice.*

❒

sensual / sensuous / sensory

Sensual and **sensuous** are often used interchangeably and we suppose there's nothing we can do about it. The difference in meanings is more one of tone than distinct definition. *Sensual* is more carnal, relating to physical appetites; "sexy." *Sensuous* tends toward esthetic pleasures and taking delight in beauty.

The two words can also intersect. Silk lingerie may be *sensuous;* but if wearing silk lingerie gets you hot then lingerie is *sensual.*

- ❑ **Sensual** excess drives out pity in man.—Marquis de Sade

- ❑ Mathematics is, as it were, a **sensuous** logic, and relates to philosophy as do the arts, music, and plastic art to poetry.—Friedrich Von Schlegel

Sensory lacks the sexy aspects of the first word and the assurance of pleasure afforded by the second. It connects most directly with the physical senses of touch, smell, taste, hearing, and seeing.

- ❑ Talent is an amalgam of high sensitivity; easy vulnerability; high **sensory** equipment (seeing, hearing, touching, smelling, tasting—intensely); a vivid imagination as well as a grip on reality; the desire to communicate one's own experience and sensations, to make one's self heard and seen.—Uta Hagen

❐

shall / will / shan't / won't

In *The American Language* (first published in 1936) H.L. Mencken wrote: "the distinction between *will* and *shall,* preserved in Standard English but already breaking down in the most correct American, has been lost entirely. *Will* has replaced *shall* completely save in the imperative. This preference extends to the inflections of both."

Michael Swan in *Practical English Usage* (1995), wrote: "British people use *I shall/I will* and *we shall/we will* with no difference in meaning in most situations." British and American usage has always differed. If you are interested, H.W. Fowler explained the proper English syntax as **shall/will/shan't/won't** as well as anyone has in *The King's English* (1908). It took him over 7300 words to do so. As Fowler admitted:

It is unfortunate that the idiomatic use, while it comes by nature to southern Englishmen (who will find most of this section superfluous), is so complicated that those who are not to the manner born can hardly acquire it; and for them the section is in danger of being useless. In apology for the length of these remarks it must be said that the short and simple directions often given are worse than useless. The observant reader soon loses faith in them from their constant failure to take him right; and the unobservant is the victim of false security.

⇨

(We wonder if *anyone* is "to the manner born" as far as language these days.)

In spoken English, the use of the 'll contractions *(I'll, we'll)* is evidently the norm on both sides of the Atlantic. You do still hear (properly) *shall* used (in first person, in question form) to express an offer. This is really a polite way of asking, "Do you want me (us) to...?" For example, *Shall I release you?* meaning "Do you want me to release you?" and *Will I release you?* meaning "Do you think I'm going to release you?"

Although very few writers adhere to them, the basic rules for formal written English are:

1. *Shall* is used to express the simple future for the first person *I* and *we*: *I shall love you forever. Will* would be used in the simple future for all other persons: *They will love you forever.*

2. In American usage, if expressing great determination, these distributions are reversed, as in: *I will have my way* or *They shall do what we ask.*

3. Using *shall* in second and third persons indicates some kind of promise about the subject *This shall be revealed to you in good time.*

As far as the negative contractions, Americans tend to use *won't* for "will not." Most rarely use *shan't.*

TANGENT: Habits & Stately Homes

When we first published a version of the *shall/will/shan't/won't* entry in our newsletter, *Writers.com,* we received a query concerning the idiom "to the manner born": "Shouldn't that be 'to the manor born'?"

The phrase is yet another example of how William Shakespeare's genius permeates the English language. (See page 60.) It is from *Hamlet* (ACT I, SCENE 4). Hamlet, Horatio, and Marcellus are on the battlements waiting for the ghost of Hamlet's father to appear. They hear the noise of Claudius's drunken revelry from inside. Horatio asks if this is a custom. Hamlet answers that it is, "But to my mind—though I am native here, and to the manner born—it is a custom more honour'd in the breach than the observance." Hamlet is not referring to his royal birth; he uses *to the manner born* to mean "accustomed to a practice or custom from birth." He is disdaining the custom (and the country's reputation) for drunkenness—even though it is his country and this is something he's seen all his life.

The idiom eventually came to have an additional meaning: "fitted by birth, rearing, long training, or experience to occupy some post or position." At some point someone wrote it "to the manor born." (*To the Manor Born* was also a popular BBC1 series that ran three seasons (1979–1981). The title was an intentional pun. This use of *manner's* homophone,

⇨

Tangent (continued)

manor, would be appropriate when meaning, as the phrase now does, "fitted to a position due to upper-class birth and education" or "born with all the advantages and opportunity that wealth brings."

Despite some dictionaries' willingness to accept *to the manor born* as a legitimate addition to standard language, we could not locate any instances where the new idiom was intentionally used.

⌐

shutter / shudder

A **shutter** is a hinged window covering or the mechanical device of a camera that opens and closes to allow light to come through the lens and expose the film.

❑ I am a camera with its **shutter** open, quite passive, recording, not thinking.—Christopher Isherwood

To **shudder** is to shiver convulsively, from fear or revulsion or to vibrate; quiver.

❑ I am unable to understand how a man of honor could take a newspaper in his hands without a **shudder** of disgust.—Charles Baudelaire

⌐

silicon / silicone

Silicon is an element found combined with oxygen in a large number of common minerals. It is a semiconductor and is the fundamental material used in making computer chips.

❑ If we hadn't put a man on the moon, there wouldn't be a **Silicon** Valley today.—John Sculley

Silicone is any of various polymeric organic silicon compounds characterized by wide-range thermal stability, high lubricity, great water repelling ability, and physiological inertness. Silicone is used in adhesives, lubricants, protective coatings, paints, electrical insulation, synthetic rubber, and prosthetic replacements for body parts. A *silicone* implant is sometimes used to increase the size of breasts.

❑ [*Baywatch*] was primarily known for two things. One on the left, and one on the right. And stuffed with **silicone**, more often than not. —Steve Tilley (*Edmonton Sun*)

TANGENT: Valley Ho!

Silicon Valley is an area in Santa Clara County, California between Palo Alto and San José known as a center for the development and manufacture of electronics and computers. The phrase *Silicon Valley* first appeared in 1971 in a series of articles that journalist Don C. Hoefler wrote for *Electronic News*, a weekly industry tabloid.

⌐

sole / soul

Sole means:

○ The only one or exclusive to one group.

❑ The **sole** meaning of life is to serve humanity.—Leo Tolstoy

○ Any of various flatfishes.

❑ Even if I set out to make a film about a fillet of **sole**, it would be about me.—Federico Fellini

○ Bottom of the foot.

❑ From the crown of his head to the **sole** of his foot, he is all mirth. —William Shakespeare

○ Underside of footwear.

❑ The workman was no cobbling clown;
A good jack boot with double **sole** he made,
To roam the woods, or through the rivers wade.—Giuseppe Giusti

Soul means:

○ The vital principle in or spiritual nature of humans.

❑ You don't have a **soul**. You are a **Soul**. You have a body.—C.S. Lewis

○ The part of one's being considered immortal.

❑ Heaven lent you a **soul**. Earth will lend a grave.—Christian Nestell Bovee

○ One human.

❑ Independence? That's middle class blasphemy. We are all dependent on one another, every **soul** of us on earth.—George Bernard Shaw

○ The vital core; essence.

❑ In books lies the **soul** of the whole past time.—Thomas Carlyle

○ A quintessential embodiment.

❑ Brevity is the **soul** of lingerie.—Dorothy Parker

○ Deep emotional or moral feeling.

❑ Love makes your **soul** crawl out from its hiding place. —Zora Neale Hurston

○ The essence of the cultural heritage of black Americans.

❑ **Soul** food is our personal passport to the past. It is much more about heritage than it is about hominy.—Sarah Ban Breathnach

❐

some day / someday

Some day is the adjective *some* plus the noun *day* meaning "one day, but not a particular day."

❑ **Some day** my prince will come...—Larry Morey

Someday is an adverb meaning "an undermined date in the future."

❑ I always say, keep a diary and **someday** it'll keep you.—Mae West

some time / sometime / sometimes

Some time is the adjective *some* plus the noun *time*.

❑ I've been trying for **some time** to develop a lifestyle that doesn't require my presence.—Gary Trudeau

Sometime can be used as an *adverb* meaning "approximately."

❑ Why don't you come up **sometime** 'n see me ?—Mae West

Sometime can be used as an *adjective* meaning either "former" or "occasional."

❑ [Here] read of the noble and joyous history of the great conqueror and excellent king, King Arthur, **sometime** King of this noble realm then called Britain...—William Caxton

Sometimes is an adverb meaning "now and then" or "occasionally."

❑ **Sometimes** I have wondered whether life wouldn't be much more amusing if we were all devils, and no nonsense about angels and being good.—William Hurlbut

The phrase **a sometime thing**, means more than "on-again-off-again." There's an implication that *sometime things* are fairly unstable.

❑ A woman is a **sometime thing**.—Du Bose Heyward

spright / sprightly / sprite

In general, the small supernatural being is a **sprite**. **Spright** is, at best a little-used or archaic variant. **Sprightly,** the adjective (or adverb) meaning "vivacious, lively, spirited," and its noun form, **sprightliness,** are based on that little-used or archaic variant *(spright)*. *Sprite* started out as a contraction of *spirit* and you will occasionally see it used as a synonym for *ghost*. The trademarked name of the lemon-lime carbonated beverage from The Coca-Cola Company is **Sprite**.

❑ Once upon a time there was a wicked **sprite**, indeed he was the most mischievous of all **sprites**.—Hans Christian Andersen

stalactites / stalagmites

Stalactites are conical mineral deposits that form on the roof of a cave and hang downward.

Stalagmites are icicle-shaped mineral deposits that form on bottom of a cave and grow upward as water drips down from above.

Always confuse the two? We bet that, like us, you learned a **mnemonic device** in order to keep them straight. (A *mnemonic device* is a formula used to aid the memory.) The problem is that there are so many different mnemonics that you still get confused. (See the *Tangent* below for a few we've found.)

You can always call them both *speleothems*. *Stalactites* and *stalagmites* are the two most common types of *speleothem*, a general term for a cave formation resulting from slow-moving water, usually containing calcium carbonate, which has been dissolved from the limestone where the cave was formed. When this water enters the cave, a chemical change occurs. The calcium carbonate hardens (precipitates), creating all types of formations.

Dripstone can also apply to both. A *stalagmite* is a post of *dripstone* growing up from a cave floor. A *stalactite* is an icicle-shaped accumulation of *dripstone* hanging from a cave roof.

When *stalagmites* and *stalactites* combine, they are called a **column**.

The earliest stage of growth of a stalactite—a long hollow translucent tube of calcite—is called a **soda straw**.

TANGENT: Mnemonic Devices That Supposedly Help You Remember the Difference Between Stalactite and Stalagmite

Warning: By the time you finish reading this list you may become confused and disoriented. Do not enter any dark caves or operate heavy equipment until this sensation passes.

○ (The) *c* in stalactite stands for ceiling and the *g* in stalagmite stands for ground.
○ Different sixth letters: stala*c*tites come from the *c*eiling, and stala*g*mites come from the *g*round.
○ Remember "ants in the pants": the mites go up and the tights come down.
○ Stalactites are hanging tightly from the ceiling and stalagmites are mighty hard and it will hurt if you trip over one.
○ Stalactites hang tight and stalagmites grow mightily.
○ Stalactites hold tight to the roof and stalagmites might one day join up with them.

⇨

Tangent (continued)

○ Stalactites must hold tightly to the ceiling lest they risk falling down. Stalagmites grow from the floor. However, given sufficient time, they might one day reach the ceiling.
○ Stalagmites (*m* for "mice") always grow on the bottom of the cave floor where mice live and stalactites (*t* is for "top") always grow on the top of the cave roof.
○ Stalagmites push up with all their might from the floor, while stalactites hold on to the ceiling really tight.
○ When the tights (tites) hang down, the mites run up.

❏

stationary / stationery

We DO have a mnemonic device to help you remember these homophones' different meanings:

Stationery is paper and other writing materials including envelopes: *e* as in envelope = *stationery*.

❑ [A logo] should look just as good in 15-foot letters on top of company headquarters as it does one sixteenth of an inch tall on company **stationery**.—Steven Gilliatt

Stationary with an *a* means "standing still, not moving."

❑ There are three classes of men; the retrograde, the **stationary** and the progressive.—Johann Kaspar Lavater

❏

stanch / staunch

Once upon a time these spellings were interchangeable, but it appears the matter is now settled in favor of different meanings. **Staunch** (*stawnch*) is used for the adjective meaning "strong and tight" (as for a ship) and, by extension, "loyal, dedicated, zealous." **Stanch** (pronounced as above or as *stanch* or somewhere in between) is used for the verb meaning "to block the flow of something."

❑ Now seek some skilful hand, whose powerful art
May **stanch** th'effusion, and extract the dart.
—Homer

❑ Build me straight, O worthy Master!
Staunch and strong, a goodly vessel...—Henry Wadsworth Longfellow

❏

straight / strait / straits

Straight means "without curves, unbending"

❑ A **straight** oar looks bent in the water. What matters is not merely that we see things but how we see them.—Michel de Montaigne.

The noun **strait** once meant "a narrow passage or space." This meaning has stayed with us to mean "a narrow channel connecting two larger bodies of water" as in the Bering Strait or the Straits of Gibraltar. **Strait(s)** can also mean "a difficult and troubled situation."

❑ Thy self bred up in poverty and **straits** at home—John Milton

As an adjective, **strait** has (according to some dictionaries) the *archaic* meaning "narrow; tight." The *current* meanings include "limited in space or time; closely fitting (constricted or tight)." The adjective form can also refer to causing distress or difficulty.

The cliché **dire straits** means "desperate circumstances or urgent need." (Mark Knopfler's band is *Dire Straits*.)

The phrase **straight and narrow**—"the way of proper and law-abiding behavior"—is sometimes written, incorrectly as **strait and narrow**. Originally the phrase was **straight and narrow path,** but due to misinterpretation of Matthew 7:14 ("Because strait is the gate, and narrow is the way which leadeth unto life...") in which **strait** means *narrow*. The phrase was sometimes mistakenly written as *strait and narrow.*

Conservative and liberal dictionaries alike approve both spellings **straitjacket** and **straightjacket.** *Straitjacket* is probably more frequently used.

Strait-laced now means "strict in behavior, opinion, and morality; narrow minded; prudish," but it comes from a literal term that meant wearing one's stays or bodice tightly laced. The supposition is that someone so constricted might have a similarly constructed view of the world. The *Tangent* below, however, has something to say about *that.*

TANGENT: What Dictionarists Apparently Do Not Know About Ladies' Apparel

We wonder just how much those who decide such things for dictionaries know about ladies' undergarments or, at least, the *history* of ladies' undergarments.

The *Oxford English Dictionary* cites four 17th century uses of *strait-laced* as the earliest use. The 17th century female (as the 16th century before) laced her torso into a lengthened tubular shape. The undergarments of the time did not cinch the waist so much as support the body and

⇨

enforce good posture. The look was not one of a small tapering waist, full breasts and hips—the "hourglass" shape—instead, the bosom was lifted and encased into a flat cylinder with an extremely full skirt. Merchant and upper class women wore stays primarily for a fashionable shape. Working women needed stays for good support. Tight lacing (*strait-* or *straight-lacing*) for vanity's sake was disapproved of.

A short bodice with tabs at the waist became the style in the 1630s and continued to be worn by the middle and lower classes through the mid-17th century. Fashionable ladies adopted a somewhat softer, rounder look by the 1630s and stays became part of the bodice itself rather than a separate undergarment. In the 1670s stays returned as a separate undergarment when wearing a patterned bodice under an over gown became the style. (Similar to the current fashion of wearing a bustier or corset as a garment to be seen.) The rigid hourglass shape reappeared in 1814 and advancing technology—the metal eyelet!—meant tighter lacing was possible.

When *strait-laced* first appeared it did not refer to one who strictly adhered to the conventional, but to those who (1) simply wore the undergarments of the day or (2) laced them—for vanity's sake—too tightly.

Even into the 19th and 20th century, the first dictionary entries were "Griped with stays" (*Webster's American Dictionary of the English Language,* 1828) and "Bound with stays." (*Webster's Revised Unabridged, 1913 Edition).*

An analogy could be drawn between the modern-day wearing of a supportive brassiere and the wearing of the average 17th century undergarment. A modern woman who wears a bra constructed to enhance her figure is analogous to the 17th century woman who was laced too tightly. Both are examples of attempts to look more sexually alluring—hardly being "strait-laced" as now defined.

❒

strategy / tactic(s)

Strategy and **tactics** are both generally used to mean "plans," but there is an important difference in meaning. In military science, *strategy* is the command, overall planning, and conduct of a war. *Tactics,* in military science, are detailed maneuvers used to achieve objectives set by strategy. For nonmilitary use, we can consider *strategy* as a long-term sytematic plan; *tactics* as smaller or day-to-day schemes. *Strategy* is the big picture, *tactics* are the little picture.

❑ **Strategy** without **tactics** is the slowest route to victory. **Tactics** without **strategy** is the noise before defeat.—Sun Tzu

❒

❧T❧

that / which

The simple (and not completely correct) rule is: Use **that** to introduce a *restrictive* (also called an *essential*) *clause*. Use **which** to introduce a *nonrestrictive* (or *nonessential*) *clause*. What are restrictive and nonrestrictive clauses? The alt.usage.english FAQ gives this example:

> "The family that prays together stays together," the clause "that prays together" is called a *restrictive clause*. It restricts the main statement to a limited class of family. In "The family, which is the basic unit of human society, is weakening," "which... society" is called a *nonrestrictive clause*. It makes an additional assertion about the family without restricting the main statement.

But the *Chicago Manual of Style* admits that this distinction is often disregarded in modern writing. Ignoring the distinction can, however, lead to confusion:

❑   The report which he had tried to suppress was greeted with gloom.

Does this mean—

❑   The report, which he had tried to suppress, was greeted with gloom.

or—

❑   The report that he had tried to suppress was greeted with gloom.

?

In general, nonrestrictive clauses should be set off by commas; restrictive clauses are not set off by commas. Nonrestrictive clauses are nearly always introduced by "which" or "who," but some experts encourage introducing restrictive clauses with "that," so copyeditors do go on "which hunts."

Veteran copyeditor Bill Walsh, in his book *Lapsing Into a Comma*, suggests remembering it this way:

> *Which* clauses are always set off—usually by a comma, but sometimes by a dash or with parentheses. So your choice is between *that* and *comma-which*. If the comma seems out of place, *that* is your answer. Of course, you can always try avoiding the issue by trying to omit object relative pronouns altogether when possible. *The book that I read* can just as properly and clearly be *the book I read*.

❒

that / who

Generally, if the subject is a human being, you use **who**. *(Women Who Run With Wolves, The Man Who Came To Dinner)* Use **that** when referring to animals or objects *(The Little Engine That Could, The Plant That Ate Dirty Socks)*.

Sometimes writers use *who* for animals with distinct personalities *(The Dog Who Had Kittens)* or are named *(Seabiscuit, the stallion who was Horse of the Year in 1938)*. Occasionally writers will use *who* when referring to corporate entities. *(We went with the firm who offered the best price.)* Some experts will accept "that" for use with people if the reference is general rather that specific. *(People that never listen never learn. Men that want only one thing usually get it.)* It can also get a little iffy when dealing with monsters and supernatural beings—are vampires, slime-monsters, and ghosts people or things?

Overall, try to go with *who* for people and *that* for everything else.

❒

their / there / they're

Their is a possessive pronoun (like *your* and *her*)

❑ The greatest evil is not done in those sordid dens of evil that Dickens loved to paint... but is conceived and ordered (moved, seconded, carried and minuted) in clear, carpeted, warmed, well-lighted offices, by quiet men with white collars and cut fingernails and smooth-shaven cheeks who do not need to raise **their** voices.—C.S. Lewis

They're is a contraction of **they are** (the apostrophe stands for the missing *a*).

❑ I think most of the people involved in any art always secretly wonder whether **they are** really there because **they're** good or there because **they're** lucky.—-Katharine Hepburn

If it is not a possessive pronoun, and it doesn't mean "they are" then use **there** (a location that is not here).

❑ Where **there** is great love, **there** are always wishes.—Willa Cather

❒

than / then

Than is a conjunction used to make comparisons or express an exception.

❑ Nothing is more fearful **than** imagination without taste.
—Johann Wolfgang von Goethe,

Then is an adverb used to indicate time.

❑ Just trust yourself, **then** you will know how to live.
—Johann Wolfgang von Goethe

❒

throes / throws

Throes are "[violent] pangs [of suffering] or struggles."

❑ The meaning of divine creation is primarily revealed in the enthusiasm of annihilation. Only in the **throes** of death is the spark of eternal life ignited.—Friedrich von Schlegel

Throws refers to throwing (hurling, flinging, propelling through air); confusing or shocking; lightweight coverings, etc.

❑ When God **throws**, the dice are loaded.—Greek proverb

❐

till / 'til / until

Till and **until** can be used interchangeably, although *until* is used especially at the beginning of a sentence and in formal style. *Till* is **not** an abbreviation of *until*. *Till*, used as a conjunction, came into use around 1130. Both have existed as prepositions meaning "up to" since about 1200. *Until* did not start being used as a preposition for "up to" until 1300.

Till comes, via Old English and Middle English, from the Old Norse word *til meaning* "to." The prefix "un-" (from Old Norse *und* meaning "up to") was added to *till* to make *until*. (We guess that makes *until* mean "up to up to.")

'Till came along in the 18th century when some misguided folks mistakenly thought *till* was a shortened version of *until*. Around 1939, more misguided folks loped off the extra *l*. Now *'til* is acceptable, *'till* is not acceptable, and, really, you're better off using *till* instead of either.

❑ There will be no end to the troubles of states, or of humanity itself, **till** philosophers become kings in this world, or **till** those we now call kings and rulers really and truly become philosophers, and political power and philosophy thus come into the same hands.—Plato

❑ Happy trails to you, **until** we meet again.
Happy trails to you, keep smilin' **until** then.—Dale Evans

❐

titillate / titivate

Titillate means "to excite someone pleasurably, superficially, or erotically."

❑ Art can excite, **titillate**, please, entertain, and sometimes shock; but its ultimate function is to ennoble.—Marya Mannes

Titivate means "to spruce up or make smart."

❑ The pied-a-terre she keeps in Rome includes a gigolo to press her pants, palpate her remote control, and **titivate** her terrazzo.
—Karen Elizabeth Gordon

❐

to / too / two

Most folks realize **two** is the number, but they do confuse **to** and **too**. *Too* is an adverb that means "also" or "in excess." If you don't mean one of those, then you must mean the preposition *to*.

❏ **Too** late, I found you can't wait **to** become perfect, you got **to** go out and fall down and get up again with everybody else.—Ray Bradbury

❏ **To** do **two** things at once is **to** do neither.—Publilius Syrus

❑

tortuous / torturous

Tortuous means "full of twists and turns or excessively lengthy and complex."

❏ So the people will pay the penalty for their kings' presumption, who, by devising evil, turn justice from her path with **tortuous** speech.—Hesiod

Torturous (the base word is *torture*) means "characterized by pain or suffering.

❏ Reason is the slow and **torturous** method by which those who do not know the truth discover it.—Blaise Pascal

❑

track / tract

Track, as a noun, can mean:

○ route, path, marked road

○ athletic competitions related to running on a track

○ the bars of rolled steel along which a vehicle can roll

○ the parallel rails along which trains travel

○ the direction in which someone's job or education develops

○ a mark or line of marks left on a surface by an animal, person or vehicle which has moved over the surface, and which shows which direction taken

○ one of several songs or pieces of music on a CD or other musical recording; part of a magnetic strip onto which sound can be recorded; groove on a sound recording consisting of a disc with continuous grooves, formerly used to reproduce music by rotating while a phonograph needle traveled in the path (tracked) in the grooves

—**and** there are a number of figurative meanings extended from the literal ones as well as related verb usages.

⇨

❑ Even if you're on the right **track**, you'll get run over if you just sit there.—Will Rogers

❑ Neither a wise man nor a brave man lies down on the **tracks** of history to wait for the train of the future to run over him.
—Dwight D. Eisenhower

❑ Cycle **tracks** will abound in Utopia.—H.G. Wells

A **tract** is a pamphlet, particularly a political or religious one, intended to influence opinion.

❑ If a theme or idea is too near the surface, the novel becomes simply a **tract** illustrating an idea.—Elizabeth Bowen

A **tract** is also

○ an extent of space, especially land

❑ A Saturday afternoon in November was approaching the time of twilight, and the vast **tract** of unenclosed wild known as Egdon Heath embrowned itself moment by moment.—Thomas Hardy

○ an extent or lapse of time

❑ My lusts they do me leave,
My fancies all be fled,
And **tract** of time begins to weave
Grey hairs upon my head.—Thomas Vaux

○ an anatomical or medical term for a bundle of nerve fibers having the same origin, function and termination or a number of organs with a common function.

❑ Ferocious beasts have a small and round stomach; their digestive **intestinal** tract is from three to five times the length of their body, when measured from mouth to anus. —E. Hering

A **Tract** is also the anthem consisting of verses of scripture (usually from the Psalms, sung) instead of the Alleluia in the mass from Septuagesima till Easter Eve.

These were called the **Tract,** from being drawn out (*tractus*) to a mournful cadence.—C. Walker

troop / troupe

A **troop** is a group or company of people, animals, or things; but it especially refers to a group of soldiers (troops = military units; soldiers). *Troop* can also mean, more specifically, "a unit of cavalry, armored vehicles, or artillery in a European army, corresponding to a platoon in the U.S. Army" or "a unit of Boy Scouts, Girl Scouts, or similar group under the guidance of an adult."

❑ The ultimate in disposing one's **troops** is to be without ascertainable shape. Then the most penetrating spies cannot pry in nor can the wise lay plans against you.—Sun Tzu

A **troupe** is also a band or collection of people, animals, or things; but it especially refers to a group of performers and associated personnel.

❑ Socialite women meet socialite men and mate and breed socialite children so that we can fund small opera companies and ballet **troupes** because there is no government subsidy.—Sugar Rautbord

❐

turbid / turgid

Turbid means "thick or opaque" OR "heavy with smoke or mist" OR "lacking in clarity or purity."

❑ The wine of youth does not always clear with advancing years; sometimes it grows **turbid**.—Carl Jung

Turgid means "tediously pompous or bombastic" OR "being in a state of distension; swollen, overflowing."

❑ The fact that the talk may be boring or **turgid** or uninspiring should not cause us to forget the fact that it is preferable to war.
—Henry Cabot Lodge Jr.

❐

❧ U ❧

unaware / unawares

The adjective **unaware** (often followed by *of*) means "not aware, unconscious."

❑ As for the author, he is profoundly **unaware** of what the classical or romantic genre might consist of.... In literature, as in all things, there is only the good and the bad, the beautiful and the ugly, the true and the false.—Victor Hugo

Unawares is an adverb and means "unexpectedly; by surprise."

❑ Religion blushing veils her sacred fires
And **unawares** Morality expires.—Alexander Pope

❑

unexceptionable / unexceptional

Unexceptionable means "not open to objection or criticism; beyond reproach."

❑ Nothing is more essential to the establishment of manners in a State than that all persons employed in places of power and trust must be men of **unexceptionable** characters.—Samuel Adams

Unexceptional means "not exceptional; ordinary."

❑ [W]e live in a routine planet of a humdrum star stuck away in an obscure corner... on an **unexceptional** galaxy which is one of about 100 billion galaxies.—Carl Sagan

❑

unique

We're going to be prescriptive, traditional, and conservative on this one: **unique** means "one of a kind, the only one." Do not describe anything as *very unique, rather unique, most unique, somewhat unique, sort of unique, fairly unique,* etc. Yes, we know *unique* has more than a single absolute sense and, as even H.W. Fowler noted, "can be modified with grace in certain uses." If you are aware of these and exceedingly comfortable in the usage—modify at will and feel superior to the rest of us who prefer not to risk it.

❑ You are **unique**, and if that is not fulfilled, then something has been lost.—Martha Graham

urban / urbane

Urban relates, in general, to cities and their characteristics.

The U.S. Census Bureau defines urban, for their specific purposes, as "comprising all territory, population, and housing units in urbanized areas and in places of 2,500 or more persons outside urbanized areas." An **urbanized area** is comprised of "one or more places ('central place') and the adjacent densely settled surrounding territory ('urban fringe') that together have a minimum of 50,000 persons. The urban fringe generally consists of contiguous territory having a density of at least 1,000 persons per square mile."

❑ The car has become the carapace, the protective and aggressive shell, of **urban** and suburban man.—Marshall McLuhan

Urbane means "suave, sophisticated, polished in manner."

❑ The differences between the two men were pronounced. [Galilei] Galileo was an **urbane** gentleman who loved wine (which he described as "light held together by moisture"), women (he had three children by his mistress, Marina Gamba), and song (he was an accomplished musician). [Johannes] Kepler sneezed when he drank wine, had little luck with women, and heard his music in the stars.—Timothy Ferris

venal / venial

Venal means "susceptible to bribery; corruptible."

❑ When all government, domestic and foreign, in little as in great things, shall be drawn to Washington as the center of all power, it will render powerless the checks provided of one government on another, and will become as **venal** and oppressive as the government from which we separated. —Thomas Jefferson

Venial, when used generally, means "forgivable, pardonable; excusable." In Roman Catholic theology a *venial* sin, unlike a *mortal* sin, does not deprive the soul of divine grace. It is a relatively slight matter or is committed without full reflection or consent. Examples include deliberate distraction at prayer, petty thievery, idleness, white lies, lack of love and generosity in small things, etc. (A mortal sin is deliberately committed and is of such serious consequence that it deprives the soul of divine grace, sins such as unbelief, hatred, adultery, serious theft, murder.)

❑ In medicine sins of commission are mortal, sins of omission are **venial**.—Theodore Tronchin

---

TANGENT: The Seven Deadly Sins

In early Church history there were various lists of especially bad sins. The list that became the standard "Seven Deadly Sins" was described by Pope Gregory (the first one) around 600 as *superbia* (pride), *invidia* (envy), *ira* (anger), *avaritia* (greed), *tristia* (sadness), *gula* (gluttony), and *luxuria* (luxury, later lust). *Tristia* was later replaced by *acedia*, or sloth (from the Greek *akedia*, meaning "not to care.") *Avaritia* is also known as "covetousness" or "avarice." To protect yourself against temptations to indulge in the Seven Deadlies, there are Seven Contrary Virtues you should practice: *humility* against pride, *kindness* against envy, *abstinence* against gluttony, *chastity* against lust, *patience* against anger, *liberality* against covetousness, and *diligence* against sloth.

---

vertex / vortex

Vertex means "the highest point, the apex." (It also has a number of specialized scientific, mathematic, or technical definitions.)

❑ And from the Ptolemies
Sand troughed us in a glittering abyss.
A serpent swam a **vertex** to the sun
On unpaced beaches leaned its tongue and drummed.—Hart Crane

A **vortex** is the hole in the midst of a whirlpool of liquid or whirlwind of air that pulls objects into its empty center. *Vortex* used figuratively to mean something or some situation that resembles a vortex.

❑ The Image is more than an idea. It is a **vortex** or cluster of fused ideas and is endowed with energy.—Ezra Pound

❒

vice / vise

(American spelling only; British and Australian spellings use **vice** for both)

Vice is (primarily) a moral weakness or an immoral activity.

❑ The inherent **vice** of capitalism is the unequal sharing of blessings; the inherent virtue of socialism is the equal sharing of miseries.
—Sir Winston Churchill

A **vise** is a clamping tool for holding objects very firmly.

❑ Nothing so concentrates the mind as having your head in a **vise**.
—Dave Wright

❒

vicious / viscous

Vicious means "dangerously aggressive, savage; marked by violence or ferocity; depraved."

❑ You may be as **vicious** about me as you please. You will only do me justice.—Richard Burton

Viscous describes a thick sticky liquid that is resistant to flowing.

❑ No man means all he says, and yet very few say all they mean, for words are slippery and thought is **viscous**. —Henry Brooks Adams

❒

waive / waiver / wave / waver

Waive means "to not demand something you are entitled to" or "not cause (a rule) to be enforced."

- ❏ Ah, take the Cash in hand and **waive** the Rest.—Edward Fitzgerald

Waiver (or **waivers**) is the act or document that gives up a right, privilege, or claim; it also means "to place (a ball player) on waivers" or "to release after placing on waivers."

- ❏ At some point, every player in baseball is put on **waivers**.—Joe Bick

Meanings for the verb **wave** include:
- ○ To motion with the hands in signal.
- ○ Flutter.
- ○ To move in waves; heave.
- ○ To become moved back and forth; brandish or flourish.
- ○ To move with a wavelike motion.
- ○ Undulate.

Meanings for the noun **wave** include:
- ○ The act of signal by a movement of the hand.
- ○ One of a series of ridges that moves across the surface of a liquid (especially across a body of water).
- ○ Something that rises rapidly and dies away.
- ○ A shape or outline having successive curves.
- ○ A movement like that of the ocean.
- ○ Curves and undulations in the hair.
- ○ A progressive disturbance propagated without displacement of the medium itself.

- ❏ There is hopeful symbolism in the fact that flags do not **wave** in a vacuum.—Arthur C. Clarke

The verb **waver** means "to sway to and fro" or "to pause in uncertainty or hold back in unwillingness."

- ❏ Grief teaches the steadiest minds to **waver**.—Sophocles

❐

wan / wane / wax

Wan (rhymes with *John*), as an adjective means "unnaturally pale, as from physical or emotional distress; suggestive or indicative of weariness, illness or melancholy; dim, barely perceptible; ineffectual."

- ❑ While the angels, all pallid and **wan**,
  Uprising, unveiling, affirm
  That the play is the tragedy "Man",
  And its hero the Conqueror Worm.—Edgar Allan Poe

[We do not know if Poe pronounced *wan* to rhyme with *man* or *man* to rhyme with *wan*.]

Wane (pronounced as *Wayne*) means "to decrease, dwindle."

- ❑ A savage place! as holy and enchanted
  As e'er beneath a **waning** moon was haunted
  By woman wailing for her demon-lover!—Samuel Taylor Coleridge

Wax (in the context of the phrase "wax and wane," not "what bees produce" or "to polish") means the opposite of *wane:* "to grow gradually larger; to increase in strength or size."

- ❑ Mankind, let us hope, will dwindle and die more contented than it ever was when it **waxed** and struggled—George Santayana

Both **wax** and **wane** are most often used to refer to the fullness of the moon, but they can and do appear in statements such as these: *His anger waxed strong and then subsided. My enthusiasm for your plan is beginning to wane.*

- ❑ Nothing that is can pause or stay;
  The moon will **wax**, the moon will **wane**,
  The mist and cloud will turn to rain,
  The rain to mist and cloud again,
  To-morrow be today. —Henry Wadsworth Longfellow

⊓

wander / wonder

Wander (among other meanings) means "to travel aimlessly."

- ❑ Not all who **wander** are lost.—J.R.R. Tolkien

Wonder (among other meanings) means "to consider or question some issue."

- ❑ Sometimes I **wonder** if men and women really suit each other.
  —Katharine Hepburn

⊓

weak / week

Weak means "lacking strength, power, force" (and has other meanings).

❑ The **weak** are more likely to make the strong **weak** than the strong are likely to make the **weak** strong.—Marlene Dietrich

A **week** is a period of seven days.

❑ A **week** is a long time in politics.—Harold Wilson

❐

wean

Wean means:

○ in the literal sense, to accustom young mammals to gain nourishment from sources other than nursing
○ in the figurative, to detach from a source of dependence, to accustom anyone to leaving an old set of circumstances or conditions
○ There is an odd, relatively new figurative sense meaning "to be raised and nourished on" as in *students **weaned** on the computer*. (Although used earlier, this was not commonly seen in print until the 1970s.) The justification of this last usage is that the process of weaning involves a substitution of some other form of nourishment: accustoming someone from one thing to another. Thus the phrase *students **weaned** on the computer* suggests the students' exposure to computers began almost as soon as they stopped nursing.

We don't care who finds this to be acceptable hyperbole, we reject it. Yes, in some instances this figurative use *does* make sense. When Alice Roosevelt Longworth said Calvin Coolidge "looks as if he had been weaned on a pickle" she was referring to a face that looked like that of a child being accustomed to a sour, strange new food." When Helen Hayes said she was "was *weaned* on grease-paint" she was accustomed to greasepaint at an extremely early age. In 1932, when a humorist wrote of babies "being *weaned* on aspirin to fortify them for the economic headaches they will certainly face," it was meant in the same sense as Helen Hayes later used it. But when Frank Sinatra said, in 1954, "I was *weaned* on the best popular music ever written," he probably meant "raised on," not "accustomed to." We feel using the phrase "weaned on" as synonymous with "raised on" is unacceptable. These examples, taken from the Web, should have used *raised* rather than *weaned*:

❑ A generation **weaned on** the legitimacy of black protest...
❑ There is a generation of computer users throughout the world that have been **weaned on** the Internet...

⇨

- ❏ [Rhythm guitarist] John worked at and was **weaned on** all the Merseybeat clubs in Liverpool...
- ❏ Gen Y, **weaned on** the technology Gen X discovered, is a market to be reckoned with.
- ❏ Some **weaned on** Star Trek might imagine other Earth-like planets with beings going about their daily lives...
- ❏ It refers to musicians **weaned on** punk...
- ❏ We were **weaned on** the "duck and cover" method of atomic weaponry survival...

Using *weaned on* in these two examples, is probably acceptable:

- ❏ Think nightmarish Dickensian street urchins **weaned on** methamphetamine and hell-bent on chaos...
- ❏ [V]astly increasing the emotional resonance for an audience **weaned on** the Bard...

However, if you mean "raised on," we suggest you use that phrase rather than "weaned on."

❒

weather / whether

Weather (primarily) refers to climate.

- ❏ You don't need a **weather** man to know which way the wind blows. —Bob Dylan

Whether is a conjunction that precedes the first of two choices.

- ❏ Morning comes **whether** you set the alarm or not.—Ursula K. LeGuin

❒

while / whilst

In British English these are interchangeable, with **whilst** probably considered the more formal. Although *whilst* pops up in American English, **while** is the most commonly used by far. In the U.S. you probably risk sounding somewhat pretentious using it.

- ❏ **While** I thought that I was learning how to live, I have been learning how to die.—Leonardo da Vinci
- ❏ It is not necessary that **whilst** I live I live happily; but it is necessary that so long as I live I should live honourably.—Immanuel Kant

❒

whiskey / whisky

❑ Tell me what brand of **whiskey** that Grant drinks. I would like to send a barrel of it to my other generals—Abraham Lincoln

❑ Logic, like **whisky**, loses its beneficial effect when taken in too large quantities.—Lord Dunsany

The original Gaelic name for the strong alcoholic distillate made from a fermented mash of grain was **usquebaug, uisgebaugh, using beatha, uisgebeatha, uisce beatha, uisge beatha,** or, well, you get the idea. Whether we spell it **whiskey** or **whisky** in English we're better off than trying the Gaelic. The Gaelic name was derived from the Latin *aqua vitae* or "water of life." (Scandinavian countries have *aquavit*, vodka started as *zhizennia voda*, some brandies or ports are called *eau-de-vie*—they all mean "water of life.") In the 18th century the Gaelic term somehow became **usky,** then *whiskey* or *whisky.*

Distinctions, at least in the U.S. (in England and Canada it's all **whisky**), in the two spellings evidently arose early in the 20th century and have not always been consistently used since then.

True **Scotch whisky**—capital *S*, lowercase *w*, and no *e* in *whisky*—is distilled in Scotland from barley that has been warmed with burning peat bricks. (This helps give it an intense smoky flavor.) Any other similar beverage made elsewhere is **whiskey** with an *e*. When referring to scotch in general it is **scotch** with a lowercase *s*.

❑ For her fifth wedding, the bride [Barbara Hutton] wore black and carried a **scotch** and soda.—Phyllis Battelle

❑

whither / wither

Whither is an adverb meaning "to what place" or "to what point, conclusion, or end."

❑ **Whither** goest thou, America, in thy shiny car in the night? —Jack Kerouac

Wither means "to become dry and sapless; to shrivel from or as if from loss of moisture." By extension it means "to lose vitality, force, or freshness."

❑ Age cannot **wither** her, nor custom stale Her infinite variety. —William Shakespeare

❑

who / whom

Most every guide to the use of **who** and **whom** will tell you it is "simple" to sort out. It is—for some people. Those familiar with German or Latin are used to dealing with case forms like *accusative* and *dative*. They probably consider *who/ whom* to be simple. For those of us who have trouble dealing with English alone, the prevalent meaning of "case forms" has something to do with a document with spaces in which to write. "Simply" explaining *Who is used for the subjective case, whereas* **whom** *is used for the objective case* doesn't fill any blanks in most of our brains.

The problem is that few of us grew up spontaneously using *whom.* Using *whom* now requires mental effort. Expending effort of any sort is not generally favored by most of us, especially writers. Some hope the linguists who claim that *whom* is "dying out" are correct and that, with a little patience, the issue can be avoided altogether. Get real. *Whom* has been officially dying now since at least 1870. The word has yet to start singing its last act aria as far as we can tell.

In daily speech and informal writing, you can use *who* most of the time. We feel that even informally, however, we should all remember to at least use *whom* after a preposition—even if people think you are strange. In formal writing you will occasionally need to use *whom,* so here are some tips.

Who is the subjective form of the pronoun (like *he/she/they*). *Whom* is the objective form (the direct or indirect object—like *him/her/them*). *Who* is used when it is the subject of the sentence and *whom* is used when it is the object.

> **Who** went to the party last night?
> (**Who** is the subject of the sentence.)
>
> That blonde **who** dated Jason was there.
> (**Who** stands for the subject of *dated Jason.*)
>
> **Who** do you think is going Friday?
> (**Who** stands for the subject of *is going Friday*)
>
> Jason forgot to **whom** he sent invitations.
> (**Whom** is the object of the preposition *to.*)
>
> Surely that blonde **whom** we all thought was a bimbo will not show up.
> (**Whom** is the object of the verb *thought.*)

Problems begin to arise with sentences like: *Whom do you want to call? Whom* is the object of *call,* so this sentence is correct. It doesn't seem "right" to us because we are used to sentences beginning with subjects rather than objects. Most people would say *Who do you want to call?* In every usage but the most formal, this colloquial exchange of *who* and *whom* is now fairly well accepted.

⇨

Another problem: With a sentence like *I saw the man whom Anna had tried to get Jennifer* to date last summer—we have to exert that mental effort and think far enough ahead to know that *whom* will be the object of the verb *date* (which is a couple of clauses away). If you were writing it you'd at least have a chance to sort it out, but chances are you aren't going to say *whom,* even if it is correct.

When in doubt, try substituting the pronoun *(he/him or she/he)* for *who/whom.* If *he* or *she* is correct, then use *who;* if it's *him* or *her,* then use *whom.* This can be easy:

>**Who/Who** called the cops?
>*He called the cops. (he=who; so—)*
>**Correct: Who** called the cops?

It can involve some word-juggling:

>Jason is the dude with **who/whom** I went clubbing with last week.
>*I went clubbing with him. (him=whom; so—)*
>**Correct:** Jason is the dude **whom** I went clubbing with last week.

This sentence's subject is separated from its subject by a clause:

>The guy standing over there (**who/whom**) is not someone I know called the police.
>*The guy ... called the police.=He called the police. (he=who; so—)*
>**Correct:** The guy standing over there **who** is not someone I know called the police

Chances are you can think of a dozen ways to avoid constructing sentences as graceless as those last two examples and avoid the *who/whom* decision altogether.

> ❑ The man **who** is a pessimist before 48 knows too much; if he is an optimist after it, he knows too little.—Mark Twain

> ❑ Those **whom** God wishes to destroy, he first makes mad.—Euripides

Note: The rules governing the use of **who** and **whom** apply equally to **whoever** and **whomever** and are ignored just as often in speech and informal writing.

❒

who's / whose

Who's is a contraction of the phrase **who is** or the phrase **who has.**

> ❑ The enemy is anybody **who's** going to get you killed, no matter which side he's on.—Joseph Heller

Whose is the possessive form of **who.**

> ❑ Never eat at a place called "Moms." Never sleep with a woman **whose** troubles are worse than your own.—William Penn

❒

widow / widower

When a man dies, his wife becomes a *widow;* when a woman dies, her husband becomes a *widower.* In obituaries, a man is *survived by his wife* or his *widow,* but a woman is *survived by her husband,* not her *widower.* We don't know why. Either *the wife of the late Mr. Dahlby* or *the widow of Mr. Dahlby* is correct, but *the widow of the late Mr. Smith* is redundant and, therefore, incorrect. People who remarry are no longer *widows* or *widowers.* Former spouses are not *widows* or *widowers.*

❑ Memory, in **widow**'s weeds, with naked feet stands on a tombstone. —Sir Aubrey de Vere

❑ Whoever marries the spirit of this age will find himself a **widower** in the next.—William Ralph Inge

❐

wreath / wreathe

Wreath [*ree*-(with the) *th* (voiced)] is a noun meaning "something entertwined into a circular shape."

❑ She wore a **wreath** of roses
The first night that we met.—Thomas Haynes Bayly

Wreathe [*ree*-(with the) *th* (unvoiced)] is a verb meaning "envelop, surround, or encircle."

❑ LAUREL, n. The *laurus,* a vegetable dedicated to Apollo, and formerly defoliated to **wreathe** the brows of victors and such poets as had influence at court.—Ambrose Bierce

❐

❧X-Y-Z❧

X ray / x ray / X-ray / x-ray

The final vote on this one still seems to be out. Unless you are using the specified style of a publication, pick one and be consistent:

- ❑ *American Heritage:* shows X both capitalized and lower-case; verb has hyphen, noun has no hyphen
- ❑ *AP:* X-ray for noun, adjective, and verb
- ❑ *Chicago Manual of Style:* x ray (noun), x-ray (adjective and verb) preferred, but variations accepted
- ❑ *Dorland's Illustrated Medical Dictionary:* x-ray
- ❑ *Guardian UK:* x-ray
- ❑ *Medlineplus Medical Dictionary:* X-ray
- ❑ *Merriam-Webster:* noun is X ray; adjective is X-ray; verb is x-ray (but notes the word is often capitalized)
- ❑ *New Fowler's Modern English Usage:* X-ray
- ❑ *New York Times:* X-ray for noun, adjective, and verb; X-Ray in headline
- ❑ *OED:* X-ray
- ❑ *Stedman's Medical Dictionary:* x-ray

Roger Corman's 1963 film starring Ray Milland is titled *X: The Man with the X-Ray Eyes* (identified as *X* in the weird opening credits).

- ❑ Do not envy the man with the **x-ray** eyes.—John Shirley

❒

yolk / yoke

A **yolk** is the yellow part of an egg.

- ❑ [H]ave you ever seen anything more revolting than an egg **yolk** breaking and spilling its yellow liquid? Blood is jolly, red. But egg **yolk** is yellow, revolting.—Alfred Hitchcock

A **yoke** is a wooden frame used to harness a team of draft animals. It has other meanings derived from its shape or use. The verb *yoke*—"to place in a yoke, to link together"—is also related to this meaning.

- ❑ Willingly no one chooses the **yoke** of slavery.—Aeschylus

❒

your / you're

Your is the possessive pronoun determiner.

- ❑ Trust **your** instincts. If you have no instincts, trust your impulses. —Noel Coward

You're is the contraction of *you are.*

❑ Just because **you're** paranoid doesn't mean they aren't after you.
—Joseph Heller

❏

ZIP code

ZIP codes are U.S. postal codes. *ZIP* is an acronym for **Zone Improvement Plan** so each letter is a capital, no periods. The word *code* is all lowercase.

TANGENT: Reading ZIP Codes

The United States Postal Service ZIP Code officially began on 1 July 1963. The first digit of the five-digit code designates a geographical region of the U.S. The numbering begins with zero for the far northeastern states and New Jersey; New York and Pennsylvania are designated with the numeral one. Continuing (more or less) down the east coast (Maryland, Delaware, Virginia. West Virginia, North and South Carolina), "two" is the designation. Georgia, Florida, Tennessee, Alabama, and Mississippi are Region Three. Kentucky, Ohio, Michigan, and Indiana constitute Region Four. Region Five takes in Wisconsin, Iowa, North and South Dakota, and Montana. The center continental states (Nebraska, Kansas, Missouri, and Indiana) are Region Six. The states south of Region Six (Oklahoma, Arkansas, Texas, and Louisiana) are "seven." Region Eight is the western states with the exception of Washington, Oregon, and California. Those three west coast states have codes starting with "nine."

The next two digits indicate a more closely pinpointed "population concentration" and center accessibility. The final two digits designate post offices or postal zones in larger zoned cities.

In 1983, the ZIP+4 code added a hyphen and four digits to the existing five-digit ZIP Code. The fifth and sixth digits denote a specific "delivery sector" (groupings of several blocks, streets, post office boxes, or office buildings; a single large office or apartment building; a small geographic area). The last two digits designate a "delivery segment" such as a single floor of an office building, one side of a street between cross streets, individual departments in a large company or institution, or a group of post office boxes.

❒

FINAL TANGENT: A (Very) Little (Abbreviated) Latin

We already mentioned you might want to avoid Latin (okay, you *should* avoid it) when writing in English (see page 144). But occasionally you just can't do without a little Latin, especially in abbreviated form. (Abbreviations are shown in parentheses.)

❑ *anno Domini (A.D.):* In the year of our Lord. A.D. does not mean "After Death." Traditionally it precedes the year (A.D. 2004), but this tradition is seldom observed. B.C., stands for "Before Christ" and thus comes after the year. C.E. is a recent term meaning "Common Era" and is used in place of A.D. B.C.E. refers to Before Common Era. C.E./B.C.E. have not yet been widely accepted. In edited American material, all usually take periods and are usually set in small caps with no spaces.

❑ *ad libitum (ad lib):* At one's pleasure.

❑ *ante meridiem (A.M.):* Before noon.

❑ *circa (c. or ca.):* About, approximately.

❑ *confer (cf.):* Compare.

❑ *curriculum vitae (c.v.):* A *curriculum vitae* is a summary of academic and professional acheivement. (Literally, it means "course of life.") *Vitae* are longer than résumés. *C.V.* are most often used for academic or research positions.

❑ *et alii (et al.):* And others.

❑ *et cetera (etc.):* And the rest.

❑ *exampli gratia (e.g.):* For the sake of, example, for instance.

❑ *floruit (fl.):* "He flourished." Used to indicate period during which a person, school, or movement was most active or flourishing.

❑ *ibidem (ibid., ib.):* In the same place.

❑ *id est (i.e.):* That is to say.

❑ *loco citato (loc. cit.):* In the place already mentioned.

❑ *nota bene (N.B.):* Mark well.

❑ *opere citato (op. cit.):* The work cited/mentioned before.

❑ *post meridiem (P.M.):* After noon.

❑ *post scriptum (P.S.):* Written later, a postscript.

❑ *quod erat demonstrandum (q.e.d):* Which was to be demonstrated.

❑ *quod vide (q.v.):* "Which see," see elsewhere.

❑ *requiscat in pace (R.I.P.):* May he rest in peace.

❑ *scilicet (sc.):* That is to say.

❑ *sic:* Thus; intentionally so. Indicates an error in a quoted source. (This is not an abbreviation.)

❑ *stet:* As it was originally. Let it stand. (This is not an abbreviation.)

❑ *versus (v., vs.):* Against.

❑ *vide:* see (This is not an abbreviation.)

❑ *videlicet (viz):* That is to say, namely. (*Technically,* there is no period. The *z* is the latin symbol for *-et,* so it is a sign of contraction, not a letter.)

❑ *vice versa (v.v.):* Turn against, conversely, the other way round.

☙*Index*☙